INTRODUCTION

The potential value of a guide to reference material
hardly needs arguing. Fifty years ago it may have been
true that students could pick up what they needed to know
during the course of their studies, but the proliferation
of new, revised, and reprinted reference works in recent
years has meant that this is certainly not so today.

There are now a considerable number of reference works
in Australian literature. Some are widely known and easily
available; others, published in obscure or unexpected
places, are less well-known and comparatively inaccessible.
Students and researchers are thus often in danger of over-
looking works which may be of material assistance in their
studies. It is also true that some reference works are more
comprehensive, or more reliable, or more convenient to use
than others. Our aim in this book has been to bring
together, describe, and evaluate the reference sources which
are most useful for the study of Australian literature.

This book is not a guide to Australian literature, or
to what has been written about it. It is strictly a guide
to sources of information. It does not contain a list of
articles on the novels of Henry Handel Richardson; it does
describe a bibliography where such a list will be found, and
the bibliographical sources that can be used to supplement
it. This book will not itself answer the numerous miscellaneous questions that arise in the course of literary study;
it does describe a selection of the works most likely to
assist in the answering of such questions. Dr Johnson
distinguished two kinds of knowledge: 'We know a subject
ourselves, or we know where we can find information upon it'.
Our concern in this book is with knowledge of the second
kind.

Chapter I is concerned with enumerative bibliography:
it describes the basic bibliographies, catalogues, finding-
lists, and indexes that will be used in compiling a checklist of references. It includes standard Australian works
such as Miller & Macartney's <u>Australian Literature : A
Bibliography</u> (2) and the <u>Australian National Bibliography</u>
(55), but naturally the greater number of its entries are
for general bibliographical aids such as the British Museum
catalogue (50) or the indexes to book reviews (74-76).

Chapter II is concerned with non-bibliographical
information: with the search for general (and especially
literary and biographical) information on subjects and
people likely to be encountered in the study of Australian

literature. Again, in each category, works of general scope,
such as the Encyclopaedia Britannica (87), and works of
specifically Australian reference, such as the Australian
Encyclopaedia (90), are brought together.

Chapter III is a guide to reference material on about
forty major Australian authors. Included are bibliographies, edited texts, textual studies, and scholarly
biographies. Excluded are autobiographies, undocumented
biographies, interviews, and critical works. The kinds of
work excluded are readily accessible through the bibliographies which are included. We have naturally chosen the
most widely-read and commonly-studied authors. The choice
of less important authors has often been determined by the
existence or lack of reference sources. This latter factor
was especially important in the selection of contemporary
writers; there seemed no point in listing an author merely
to announce the absence of a bibliography. References to
many authors not treated in this chapter will be found in
Chapter V; the gaps disclosed here should act as a stimulus
to further research on authors neglected or inadequately
documented.

Chapter IV describes the most important current periodicals in the field of Australian literature and literary
studies, and is therefore both a guide to an important kind
of resource and a directory of publishing opportunities.
Also listed here are general surveys of Australian literary
magazines.

Chapter V is a summary guide to strengths, particularly
in collections of Australian literary manuscripts, of the
most important Australian research libraries with holdings
in this field. The entries are based on information supplied
by the various libraries. The availability of primary
material is often a crucial factor in research; this
information may be particularly helpful to students selecting
thesis topics.

Chapter VI describes a selection of standard works on
literary study as a discipline and on its most important
branches, providing both a guide to methodology and an
intellectual context for the study of Australian literature.

The precise scope and detailed organization of the
book will be clear from the analytical table of contents
and from the headnotes to each chapter and most sections.
The order of entries has been determined by the internal
logic of a section. Readers should begin by studying the
table of contents. Rapid access to items on particular
authors or subjects is provided by the Index. Authors are
indexed comprehensively, whether their names occur in
entries or in annotations. Titles and subjects are indexed
selectively. Titles are indexed when there is no author
(e.g. Index to Australian Book Reviews, 7), and in other

AUSTRALIAN BIBLIOGRAPHIES

GENERAL EDITOR

Grahame Johnston

AUSTRALIAN LITERATURE
– a reference guide

FRED LOCK and ALAN LAWSON

MELBOURNE

OXFORD UNIVERSITY PRESS

LONDON WELLINGTON NEW YORK

Oxford University Press

OXFORD LONDON GLASGOW NEW YORK
TORONTO MELBOURNE WELLINGTON CAPE TOWN
IBADAN NAIROBI DAR ES SALAAM LUSAKA ADDIS ABABA
KUALA LUMPUR SINGAPORE JAKARTA HONG KONG TOKYO
DELHI BOMBAY CALCUTTA MADRAS KARACHI

© *Fred Lock and Alan Lawson 1977*

First published 1977

NATIONAL LIBRARY OF AUSTRALIA CATALOGUING IN
PUBLICATION DATA

Lock, Fred.
    Australian literature.

    (Australian bibliographies).
    Index.
    Bibliography.
    ISBN 0 19 550538 7.

    1. Australian literature—Bibliography.
    I. Lawson, Alan John, joint author. II. Title.
    (Series).

    016.82

PRINTED IN HONG KONG BY HING YIP PRINTING COMPANY LTD.
PUBLISHED BY OXFORD UNIVERSITY PRESS, 7 BOWEN CRESCENT, MELBOURNE

cases where a work is commonly known by its title rather
than by its author or editor (e.g. Cumulated Fiction Index,
14). Unhelpful titles are not indexed: thus the British
Museum General Catalogue of Printed Books (50) is indexed
as British Museum catalogue, not General Catalogue.
Specific subjects (e.g. Drama) are indexed when they assist
in locating entries not readily findable through the table
of contents. General subjects (e.g. Australian literature),
subjects that comprise a section of the book (e.g. theses),
and simple cross-references, are not indexed. All internal
cross-referencing is by entry number. The great majority
of references in the index are also entry-numbers, but there
are some page references to the headnotes. Authors as
subjects will be found in the author-index.

An important part of our purpose in this book has been
to annotate every item, not merely to list references. The
annotations are in part descriptive and in part evaluative,
noting scope, scale, reliability, up-to-dateness, and ease
of use. The scale of annotation naturally varies: a
standard source can often be described more concisely than
one of more doubtful status, so that annotation is not
always proportionate to the importance of the work. We have
often made comparative evaluations of similar, complementary,
or overlapping sources, sometimes enabling the reader to
select the work most useful for his purpose, at other times
making the point that two or more works must be consulted.
Two or more related works are sometimes described in a single
note. In Chapter III some important series are described
collectively at the beginning of the chapter; individual
items are annotated as well, but the reader should refer back
to the general comments (pp. 36-37).

Most (but inevitably not all) of the works described
here are ones that we have used in the course of our own
studies and research, but in no case have we described a
work that we have not at least examined. Where we know of
new or revised editions, forthcoming or in preparation, of
works included, we have mentioned them in the annotations,
but we have excluded new works in preparation. Our purpose
has been to represent the existing state of reference
sources, and those that may reasonably be expected to
appear during the currency of this edition, not to record
work in progress or planned. All bibliographies are soon
out of date, and this will be no exception; it represents
the state of our knowledge at the end of June 1976. In
one case (307) a new edition known but not available to us
at the time of writing is noted; others that we list as
forthcoming will no doubt have appeared before this book
is published.

Theses have been excluded, in some cases reluctantly.
The Australian Union List (63) is far in arrears, and it
would have been impossible for us to have examined all the
theses that may contain reference material.

In bibliographical citations we have followed the
degressive principle, describing a main-entry fully, but
giving abbreviated references to supplements (which are
generally shelved alongside their parent works) and to
works not given separate entries. We hope to have given
sufficiently full bibliographical details to enable readers
to find all publications quickly and easily in their
library. But to conserve space we have excluded information
of largely historical interest, such as details of editions
intermediate between the first and the latest. We have
always given the date of first publication, however, believ-
ing this to be a piece of information of some importance.
Serial publications often change their name, place of publication, publisher, or frequency; sometimes several of these
have varied over a long publishing history. We record the
year of first publication, but the other details given are
the current ones. Whenever such changes seemed likely to
cause confusion, or to make a work difficult to find, as
with the name-changes of <u>Who's Who in Australia</u> (113), we
have recorded important variants.

It is a pleasure to record our thanks to Spencer Routh,
Marianne Ehrhardt, Grahame Johnston, and Laurie Hergenhan
who read the work in typescript and made many valuable
suggestions. We are also grateful to the librarians who
supplied us with information about their holdings for
Chapter V.

Since this is a selective bibliography, 'omissions' will
often be a matter of opinion and personal choice but we will
be glad to receive comments and suggestions. If errors have
crept in, as they are sure to have done, corrections will be
gratefully and penitently received. Our aim has been to
produce a book that will be useful to readers and students
of Australian literature, and we will welcome any opportunity
of making it more useful and more accurate.

St Lucia   Fred Lock

4 July 1976   Alan Lawson

ABBREVIATIONS

A & R	Angus and Robertson
ABC	Australian Broadcasting Commission
ALS	Australian Literary Studies
AWW	Australian Writers and Their Work
ed.	edited by
edn	edition
eds	jointly edited by
NLA	National Library of Australia
no.	number
nos	numbers
OUP	Oxford University Press
rev.	revised (by)
TWAS	Twayne's World Authors Series
vol.	volume
vols	volumes

CONTENTS

Page

I   BIBLIOGRAPHICAL AIDS

Bibliographies range from selective reading-lists to exhaustive compilations that aim at completeness within a chosen area. Almost every kind of literary study, and all research, requires a bibliography of some kind. Some bibliographies describe the physical make-up of the books they include. Works dealing with this kind of 'analytical' bibliography will be found in Chapter VI. Bibliographies that are simply lists of references are often called 'checklists' to distinguish them from analytical bibliographies. The making of checklists is called 'enumerative' bibliography. This chapter is itself an annotated checklist of the works that will be found most useful in compiling a checklist on an Australian literary subject.

For many purposes the sources described in 'Starting points' (1-4) will suffice. When greater comprehensiveness is required, they should be supplemented by the 'Serial bibliographies'. (5-10) and by the 'Special bibliographies and aids' (11-33). Where completeness is desired, a thorough search will need to be made using the works described in 'Location aids and finding lists' (44-86).

In research it is never wise to rely entirely on an existing bibliography. Even if its scope is adequately and accurately defined, in practice its contents may have been influenced by its compiler's sense of relevance, or limited by the resources available. Brief and ephemeral items are particularly likely to have been excluded, yet they may be important for some other purpose.

A   Starting points

The first task in any literary study or research is usually to compile a checklist of both primary sources (the works that are the object of the study) and secondary sources (what has already been written about the subject). In Australian literature four works are particularly useful in this preliminary search: Miller (1), Miller & Macartney (2), Johnston (3), and Hergenhan (4). Their particular uses and limitations are discussed below, but a brief comparative evaluation can profitably be given first.

For an overview of an historical period, Miller and Johnston are best. Johnston is less detailed but more up-to-date and easier to use. Both are arranged chronologically but bring together an author's work either

in an index (Johnston) or through one (Miller). Miller &
Macartney provides the best listing of an author's works
together with brief biographical and critical information.
Hergenhan includes very many fewer authors than the others,
but for the authors he does include he offers a good
selective listing, in one place, of both primary and
secondary sources. When the forthcoming revision is
published, Hergenhan will also be the most up-to-date of
the four.

1   MILLER, E. MORRIS. Australian Literature from Its
    Beginnings to 1935 : A Descriptive and Bibliograph-
    ical Survey of Books by Australian Authors in Poetry,
    Drama, Fiction, Criticism and Anthology with
    Subsidiary Entries to 1938. 2 vols. Melbourne
    University Press, Melbourne, 1940. Facsimile edn
    with addendum of corrections and additions. Sydney
    University Press, Sydney, 1975.

    This is not a conveniently organized book. The main
    author-entry is a biographical and critical intro-
    duction with references to works by and about the
    author. The bibliographies are arranged by genre.
    All of an author's works in a genre are listed under
    the date of his first book in that genre. An author's
    total output is never brought together, nor are
    secondary works listed in one place: references must
    be assembled through the 'General Index'. The
    'Subject Index to Fiction' may also be useful, as may
    the appendix of 'Non-Australian Authors of Novels
    Associated with Australia'. For other subject-indexes
    to fiction, see (14, 128).

2   MILLER, E. MORRIS & MACARTNEY, FREDERICK T.
    Australian Literature : A Bibliography to 1938 by
    E. Morris Miller, Extended to 1950 with an Historical
    Outline and Descriptive Commentaries by Frederick T.
    Macartney. A & R, Sydney, 1956.

    A re-arranged, updated, and condensed version of
    Miller (1), which in some details remains the more
    accurate work. The great advantage of this revision
    is its ease of use: authors are listed in a single
    alphabetical sequence. A separate Corrigenda was
    issued after publication.

3   JOHNSTON, GRAHAME. Annals of Australian Literature.
    OUP, Melbourne, 1970.

    A chronological conspectus of Australian literature,
    listing for each year (1789-1968) the principal
    publications and notable literary events. The index
    is particularly convenient for quick reference: it
    includes (with dates) books by and about an author,
    and major periodicals. In the annals the main
    entries note genre, series, reprints, editions,
    pseudonyms, and collaborations. Not strictly a
    bibliography but an accurate and easy to use
    reference work. For more recent creative writing

see the annual bibliographies in <u>ALS</u> (5) and
<u>Journal of Commonwealth Literature</u> (6).

4   HERGENHAN, L.T.   'Bibliographical Appendix'.   <u>The</u>
     <u>Literature of Australia</u>.   Ed. Geoffrey Dutton.
     Penguin, Ringwood, 1964.

     This has been extensively revised and updated for a
     new edition (forthcoming 1976).   It will include
     'Bibliographical and Reference Aids', a selection of
     'General Studies', and separate entries for important
     authors with biographical notes, a list of works and
     selected 'self-commentaries' and criticism.   The
     entries are rarely annotated.   'General Histories',
     'The Social Background and Contemporary Scene',
     'Biographies, Autobiographies, Memoirs, Reminiscences
     and entries for some minor authors, all included in
     the first edition, will be omitted from the revision.

B   Serial bibliographies

     These bibliographies are especially useful for finding
recent books, articles, and reviews.   They can also be used
to update earlier bibliographies or to supplement selective
ones.   Where none exists a preliminary checklist can be
compiled from these serial bibliographies.

5   'Annual Bibliography of Studies in Australian
     Literature'.   <u>ALS</u>, 1964- .   Annual in May issue.

     Lists books, articles, and reviews of the preceding
     year.   Since 1968 the bibliography has been compiled
     in the Fryer Library (300).   There are two sections:
     'General', and 'Individual Authors'.   The listing of
     reviews is selective;   reviews of unpublished plays
     were excluded before 1974.   This bibliography is the
     most comprehensive and reliable guide to critical
     and scholarly writing on Australian authors and
     subjects and to the more important works on
     Australian English.   This is certainly the
     bibliography to consult first but for a fuller
     listing of new creative writing and reviews, it can
     be supplemented by the 'Annual Bibliography' in
     <u>Journal of Commonwealth Literature</u> (6).

6   'Australia'.   'Annual Bibliography of Commonwealth
     Literature'.   <u>Journal of Commonwealth Literature</u>,
     1965- .   Annual in December issue.

     Supplements the <u>ALS</u> 'Annual Bibliography' (5) for
     new creative writing, current serials, anthologies,
     and non-fiction.   Separate listing of reference aids;
     gives book prices;   short introductory critical
     survey.

7   <u>Index to Australian Book Reviews</u>. Libraries Board
     of South Australia, Adelaide, 1965- . Quarterly;
     annual cumulation in December issue.

     Indexes reviews and articles from about sixty
     Australasian journals, including the major newspapers.
     Includes reviews of books by Australians, originating
     in Australia, or of Australian interest. There are
     indexes of titles and of reviewers. Publication
     is currently in arrears. Also contains annual
     supplements to the Bibliographies of Australian
     Writers published by the Libraries Board, though for
     these authors it is wise to check the author entry
     in the <u>Index</u> as well.

8   <u>Annual Bibliography of English Language and Literature</u>.
     Modern Humanities Research Association, Cambridge,
     1921- . '<u>MHRA</u>'.

9   <u>MLA International Bibliography of Books and Articles</u>
     <u>on the Modern Languages and Literatures</u>. Modern
     Language Association of America, New York, 1957-
     Annual. Published as part of <u>PMLA</u> until 1968.
     '<u>MLA</u>'.

     The two standard serial bibliographies of English
     studies. <u>MHRA</u> includes reviews of books listed, but
     not dissertations or their abstracts. <u>MLA</u> excludes
     reviews but includes published abstracts of
     dissertations. <u>MHRA</u> has no Australian section but
     Australian authors are included in the chapters on
     the nineteenth and twentieth centuries. <u>MLA</u> has an
     Australian section but it is arranged by author of
     book or article and is not indexed. Less inclusive
     and less informative than <u>ALS</u> (5), it is most
     useful for 1958-64 and for the occasional item missed
     by <u>ALS</u>. The <u>MLA</u> also publishes a companion volume of
     <u>Abstracts</u>; in their present form they are less useful
     than <u>AES</u> (10).

10   <u>Abstracts of English Studies</u>. Boulder, Colorado,
     1958- . Monthly, September to June. '<u>AES</u>'.

     Much more selective than either the <u>MLA</u> (8) or
     <u>MHRA</u> (9) annual bibliographies, but each entry is
     given a brief abstract. The editors of AES select
     the books and articles to be abstracted, and the
     abstracts are written by <u>AES</u> contributors. In the
     <u>MLA</u> system, the abstracts are written by the authors
     of the articles, and participating journals
     contribute abstracts of all their articles.
     Australian literature is included, and most of the
     Australian literary periodicals are abstracted.
     Indexed in each number and cumulatively for each
     year.

C   Special bibliographies and aids

i   Fiction

11   WRIGHT, R. GLENN (ed.). Author Bibliography of
     English Language Fiction in the Library of Congress
     through 1950. 8 vols. Hall, Boston, 1973.

     The 'Australian Authors' section includes about
     1,200 books by authors who published their first
     novel before 1951. The latest entries are for
     1970. Volume 7 contains an index of pseudonyms.

12   HUBBLE, GREGORY VALENTINE. The Australian Novel :
     A Title Checklist 1900-1970. The author, Perth,
     1970.

     Merely a listing by title of novels by Australian
     authors in the period. There is no index and no
     introduction. Clearly much less useful than
     Johnston's Annals (3). Its only use is for
     identifying the author of a book known only by
     title.

13   HUBBLE, G.V. Modern Australian Fiction : A
     Bibliography, 1940-1965. The author, Perth, 1968.

     An author-checklist of 1940 to 1965 imprints,
     marred by numerous and serious errors and
     omissions, and by a failure to refer to pre-1940
     imprints of books listed.

14   COTTON, G.B. & GLENCROSS, ALAN (eds). Cumulated
     Fiction Index 1945-1960. Association of Assistant
     Librarians, London, 1960. Two supplements cover
     1960 to 1974.

     A useful subject-index: in the main volume, about
     25,000 titles are classified under about 3,000
     headings. Not limited to fiction published within
     the terminal dates; includes classics and other
     works 'current' in British public libraries during
     the period. About 180 Australian authors are
     represented.

15   COOK, DOROTHY & MONRO, ISABEL S. Short Story Index.
     Wilson, New York, 1953. Five Supplements cover
     1950 to 1973. Now annual.

     The main volume indexes by author, title, and
     subject about 60,000 stories in 4,320 collections
     (there is an author/title-index of these). Does
     not include stories published in periodicals, but
     does include single-author collections.

ii   Poetry

16   SERLE, PERCIVAL. Bibliography of Australasian
     Poetry and Verse, Australia and New Zealand.
     Melbourne University Press, Melbourne, 1925.

     Describes 2,700 volumes by 1,420 authors; slightly
     fuller information than Miller (1) or Miller &
     Macartney (2).

17   HORNIBROOK, J.H. Bibliography of Queensland Verse,
     with Biographical Notes. Government Printer,
     Brisbane, 1953.

     Comprehensive for 1868-1949 with some entries to 1952.
     Also lists serials and critical works (but without
     cross-references to poets discussed). Identifies
     many pseudonyms including several not in Nesbitt &
     Hadfield (25). More detailed than Miller (1) or
     Miller & Macartney (2).

18   CUTHBERT, E.I. Index of Australian and New Zealand
     Poetry. Scarecrow Press, New York, 1963.

     An author-index to twenty-two anthologies (including
     three annuals). Also indexes titles and first
     lines.

19   SMITH, WILLIAM JAMES (ed.). Granger's Index to
     Poetry. 6th edn. Columbia University Press, New
     York, 1973. 1st edn 1904.

     Main section indexes by title and first line 514
     anthologies; there are also indexes to authors and
     subjects.

20   EDWARDS, RON. Index to 1972 : Australian Folk Song.
     Rams Skull Press, Holloway Beach, Qld, 1973 .

     An annotated finding-list, arranged by title.
     Annotation includes first line, and often, tune,
     author and alternate titles. About forty
     collections and periodicals are indexed. There is
     also an index to first lines.

21   A Bibliography of Songs and Folk-lore of Australia :
     Preliminary Draft. NLA, Canberra, 1965.

     A checklist of anthologies of Australian song; the
     folk-lore list is too brief to be useful.

iii Drama

Australian drama has probably received less than its due attention from critics, literary historians and compilers of reference works alike. As a great many plays remain unpublished, guides to collections such as the Campbell Howard (23) and Hanger (24) are particularly important.

22   HO, E.F. Australian Drama, 1946-1973 : A Bibliography of Published Works. State Library of South Australia Reference Services Bibliographies. Libraries Board of South Australia, Adelaide, 1974.

An author-checklist of about 200 plays; lists anthologies under editor. Notes number of acts, characters, theme, setting, etc. Supplement with Rees (127) especially for 1936-46 and for broadcast plays.

23   APTED, S.M. Australian Plays in Manuscript : A Check List of the Campbell Howard Collection Held in the University of New England Library. Preface by Campbell Howard. University of New England Library, Armidale, 1968.

About 200 Australian plays, performed but (with a few exceptions) unpublished, 1920-55. Contains several plays previously thought lost. Copies of the scripts are now also held in NLA. Most of the plays are typescripts, not holographs.

24   Hanger Collection : Bibliography of Play Scripts. Fryer Library, University of Queensland, St Lucia, 1975.

Author-checklist of the largest collection of Australian playscripts, giving date (where known) and number of acts. Broadcast plays are identified as such. About 600 plays are listed but the collection is still growing; many playwrights regularly deposit copies of their scripts.

iv Special topics

25   NESBITT, BRUCE & HADFIELD, SUSAN. Australian Literary Pseudonyms : An Index with Selected New Zealand References. Libraries Board of South Australia, Adelaide, 1972.

Identifies pseudonyms and lists, under the real name, all an author's known pseudonyms. Does not give its sources for attributions, though most derive from Miller & Macartney (2). Incomplete but a good starting point; see also Halkett & Laing (26).

26   HALKETT, SAMUEL & LAING, JOHN. Dictionary of
      Anonymous and Pseudonymous English Literature.
      Enlarged edn by James Kennedy & others. 9 vols.
      Oliver & Boyd, Edinburgh, 1926-62.

      'English' means written in, or translated into,
      English. Inconvenient to use because of its
      several sequences, and marred by its failure to
      quote its authorities for attributions. These
      defects will be remedied in a new edition which is
      in preparation.

27   MUIR, MARCIE. A Bibliography of Australian
      Children's Books. Deutsch, London, 1970.

      Bibliographical descriptions of children's books
      relating to Australia or written by Australian
      authors. There are, however, some odd exclusions
      and errors. The definition of children's book in
      the 'Introduction' should be consulted. Appended is
      a 'Select Bibliography of the South West Pacific
      Area'. See also Saxby (129).

28   LAIRD, J.T. 'A Checklist of Australian Literature of
      World War I'. ALS, vol. 4, no. 2, October 1969,
      pp. 148-63.

      Arranged by author within three sections : 'Verse',
      'Fiction', and 'Personal Narratives'. Excludes
      anthologies. Identifies a number of pseudonyms.
      Includes works about the War whenever published
      (the latest entry is 1965).

29   BLAIR, DAVID. 'A Bibliography of Australian English'.
      English Transported : Essays on Australasian
      English. Ed. W. S. Ramson. Australian National
      University Press, Canberra, 1970.

      The bibliography has five subject-divisions,
      arranged alphabetically by author, and an index.
      Reviews and theses are included and there is some
      annotation. An accurate and comprehensive guide to
      a subject of frequent relevance to literary studies.

30   SEGERSTRÖM, HENRY. Australiska och Nyzeeländska
      Författare på Svenska, 1830-1974. Litteratur-
      orientering och Bibliografi vid Bibliotekshögskolan,
      Borås, 1975.

      A comprehensive checklist of Swedish translations
      of Australian and New Zealand literature and of
      secondary material in Swedish. The main section is
      arranged by authors. The list of general articles
      notes authors and subjects covered. Children's
      books, films, and plays are also included.

31 FARMER, GEOFFREY. Private Presses and Australia, with a Check-List. Hawthorn Press, Melbourne, 1972.

A survey of private presses in Australia, followed by a list of private presses and their owners and a comprehensive checklist of private press-publications listed under the name of the press-owner.

32 HANNAFORD, C.H. Index to 'The Lone Hand': May 1907-November 1913. Libraries Board of South Australia, Adelaide, 1967.

Indexes of authors, titles, and subjects.

33 WOODHOUSE, MARGARET. An Index to 'The Stockwhip', 1875-1877, with a Life of John Edward Kelly, 1840-1896. Margaret Woodhouse, Sydney, 1969.

Poems are indexed by author under 'Poetry'; little else of literary interest. Kelly edited The Stockwhip.

D   Guides to reference sources

34 WALFORD, A.J. (ed.). Guide to Reference Material. 3rd edn. 3 vols. Library Association, London, 1973- . Vols 1 & 2 published; vol. 3 in preparation. 1st edn 1959; 2nd edn of vol. 3 (Generalities, Languages, the Arts and Literature) 1970.

The most useful listing of general reference sources. Although British in emphasis, it contains more Australian items than Winchell (35). Annotations indicate the scope of each work listed, and often add helpful evaluative comments. The lack of a general index makes it difficult to locate works in areas that overlap the humanities and social sciences.

35 WINCHELL, CONSTANCE M. Guide to Reference Books. 8th edn. American Library Association, Chicago, 1967. Three Supplements by Eugene P. Sheehy, 1968-72. 1st edn 1902.

The American equivalent of Walford (34), but less convenient to use. The main volume extends only to 1964; each supplement covers only a two-year period; and there is no cumulative index. Walford is certainly the one to consult first, but Winchell's American emphasis is often an advantage.

36 American Reference Books Annual. Libraries Unlimited, Littleton, Colorado, 1971- . Annual. Index, 1970-74, 1974. 'ARBA'.

Reviews reference books published or distributed in

the United States; many of the reviews offer
useful comparative evaluations. A convenient way
of keeping up with recent works.

37   ALTICK, RICHARD D. & WRIGHT, ANDREW. Selective
Bibliography for the Study of English and American
Literature. 5th edn. Macmillan, New York, 1975.
1st edn 1960.

A useful reference guide for students. There is a
good introduction, but few entries are annotated.
For a fuller treatment of American literature, see
Gohdes (38).

38   GOHDES, CLARENCE. Bibliographical Guide to the
Study of the Literature of the U.S.A. 3rd edn.
Duke University Press, Durham, 1970. 1st edn 1959.

More detailed than Altick & Wright (37). Most
entries are annotated.

39   Australian Bibliography and Bibliographical Services.
Australian Advisory Council on Bibliographical
Services (AACOBS), Canberra, 1960. 'ABBS'.

A bibliography of reference works and services;
arrangement is by type (e.g. library catalogues)
and subject. Now seriously out-of-date, but a new
edition is in preparation.

40   BORCHARDT, D.H. Australian Bibliography : A Guide
to Printed Sources of Information. 2nd edn.
Cheshire, Melbourne, 1966. 1st edn 1963.

Treats Australian bibliographical sources in seven
discursive chapters. Every work cited is discussed.
Bibliographical references are collected at the end,
and there is an index of subjects. A valuable and
comprehensive treatment of Australian reference
works. An enlarged edition is forthcoming (Pergamon
Press, Rushcutter's Bay, 1976).

41   BESTERMAN, THEODORE. A World Bibliography of
Bibliographies. 4th edn. 5 vols. Societas
Bibliographica, Lausanne, 1965-66. 1st edn 1949-50.

Lists about 117,000 separately-published bibliographies, classified by subject; indexed, but no
annotations.

42   Bibliographic Index : A Cumulative Bibliography of
Bibliographies. Wilson, New York, 1948- . Twice
yearly; annual cumulation. Larger cumulations for
1937-68.

Unlike Besterman (41), includes bibliographies
published as parts of other works. Arranged by
subject; no author-index.

43   HOWARD-HILL, T.H. <u>Bibliography of British Literary</u>
      <u>Bibliographies</u>. Clarendon Press, Oxford, 1969.
      A good finding-list for miscellaneous bibliographies;
      most items are helpfully annotated. The subjects
      covered (e.g. Tobacco) are neither all literary nor
      exclusively British.

E   <u>Location aids and finding-lists</u>

                    i Books

     The first place to look for a book is obviously the
catalogue of one's own institutional library. But during
the course of research it will often be necessary to use
other location aids, such as published library catalogues,
national bibliographies, and publishers' trade-lists.
Because almost all English-language books are either
published or distributed in the United States, American
bibliographical sources are the most comprehensive and
should (except for books originating in Australia) be
consulted first.

     The National Library of Australia receives, under
copyright legislation, a copy of each book published in
Australia. The <u>Australian National Bibliography</u> (55) is
basically the record of this copyright intake. In the
United States the deposit library is the Library of
Congress, which publishes the <u>National Union Catalog</u> (47).
This is broader in scope than a national bibliography; it
is a general record of new imprints acquired by American
libraries, wherever published. For the United Kingdom there
is the <u>British National Bibliography</u> (51), compiled at the
British Library (formerly the British Museum Library).

     Apart from these current listings, each country also
has a retrospective record of national library holdings.
The largest of these is the <u>National Union Catalog: Pre-</u>
<u>1956 Imprints</u> (44). There is no equivalent British union-
list, although there is a catalogue of the country's
largest library, the British Library (50). Australia is
served by <u>NUCOM</u> (52), a card-catalogue soon to be published
on microfilm. All three of these are comprehensive in
scope; they are not limited to books originating in their
own country.

     Of narrower scope are the retrospective national
bibliographies, or bibliographical records of books
published within the country (and usually of other books
of national interest, variously defined). Of these only
the Australian one is of interest here: Ferguson's
<u>Bibliography of Australia</u> (54). To complement Ferguson and
the serial <u>Annual Catalogue of Australian Publications</u> (now

the Australian National Bibliography), an Australian
National Bibliography 1901-1950 is being compiled.

Trade-lists can usefully supplement library catalogues
and national bibliographical records. They often record
more completely such items as reprints and new editions of
fiction. Probably the most useful current listing is the
Cumulative Book Index (49). An important source for the
nineteenth century (when much Australian literature was
published in England) is the English Catalogue of Books
(London, 1801- ; but less useful after 1924).

Two classes of material largely ignored by these aids
are government publications and foreign-language books.
Neither is sufficiently important in the study of Australian
literature to be treated in detail here, but we have
described two useful finding-lists (56, 57).

44   The National Union Catalog: Pre-1956 Imprints.
     Mansell, London, 1968- . About 450 vols published
     (to P); to be completed in about 610 vols. 'NUC:
     Pre-1956 Imprints'.

     When completed (by about 1978) will be the most
     comprehensive published record of printed books,
     containing an estimated thirteen million entries.
     For most authors and subjects involving predominantly
     books printed after about 1800, this is the best
     starting-point. The entries are photographed
     library cards. Six major American research libraries
     reported their total holdings; most other American
     (and some Canadian) research libraries reported
     selectively titles they believed not to be widely
     held. The bibliographical standard of the catalogue
     cards varies a good deal between libraries for books
     not represented by standard Library of Congress
     cards. Among the best are those originating at
     Harvard (MH). But reprints, reissues, and new
     editions are not always properly distinguished..

45   A Catalog of Books Represented by Library of Congress
     Printed Cards Issued to July 31 1942. 167 vols.
     Edwards, Ann Arbor, 1942-46.

     Still useful pending the completion of NUC: Pre-1956
     Imprints (44). Unlike the NUC, it is limited to
     books held in the Library of Congress.

46   Library of Congress and National Union Catalog Author
     Lists, 1942-1962: A Master Cumulation. 152 vols.
     Gale, Detroit, 1969.

     From 1942 to 1952, a record of acquisitions of new
     books by the Library of Congress, and therefore a
     continuation of its catalogue (45). From 1952
     includes not only titles held in the Library of
     Congress but others reported to the National Union

Catalog (47). For books published before 1956,
NUC: Pre-1956 Imprints (44), where published, is
a more comprehensive source.

47   The National Union Catalog: A Cumulative Author
     List. Library of Congress, Washington, 1956- .
     Monthly; quarterly, annual, and five-yearly
     cumulations. 'NUC'.

     The most comprehensive current listing. For books
     published in 1962 or earlier consult the Master
     Cumulation (46).

48   The Library of Congress Catalog . . . Books:
     Subjects. Library of Congress, Washington, 1950-
     Quarterly; annual and five-yearly cumulations.

     The most useful subject-index. The headings used
     in the Library of Congress (and by other libraries
     that have adopted the Library of Congress
     classification system) are listed in Library of
     Congress Subject Headings (8th edn, Washington, 1975).
     Finding the right entries to consult can save much
     time and angst.

49   Cumulative Book Index: A World List of Books in the
     English Language. Wilson, New York, 1900- .
     Monthly (except August); quarterly and annual
     cumulations. Larger cumulations before 1969. 'CBI'.

     The most useful current trade-list: authors, titles,
     and subjects in a single sequence. Less compre-
     hensive before 1928. For British books, consult also
     Whitaker's Cumulative Book List (London, 1924- ;
     monthly with cumulations).

50   BRITISH MUSEUM. General Catalogue of Printed Books:
     Photolithographic Edition to 1955. 263 vols.
     Trustees of the British Museum, London, 1959-66.
     Ten-Year Supplement 1956-65, 50 vols, 1968.
     Five-Year Supplement 1966-70, 26 vols, 1971-72.

     A major reference tool, recording the holdings of
     the largest British library. Basically an author-
     catalogue; there are subject-entries for authors
     and for some other proper names, but the latter are
     erratic and unreliable. The treatment of pseudonyms,
     and of authors who changed their names during the
     course of their careers, is idiosyncratic and can be
     annoying. Anonymous works are entered under a proper
     name, if there is one in the title. Especially
     useful for books printed before 1800, for which its
     superior standard of cataloguing is a decided
     advantage. For modern books, it is a less compre-
     hensive record than NUC Pre-1956 Imprints (44),
     being weak on American imprints and on reprints.
     The terminal dates of the two Supplements refer to
     acquisitions by the library; both contain very

large numbers of books printed before 1956. A more
complete record of recent British books is the
British National Bibliography (51).

51   The British National Bibliography. British Library,
London, 1950- . Weekly; four-monthly and annual
cumulations. Larger cumulations before 1971. 'BNB'.

The most comprehensive record of books published in
Britain, although it excludes certain kinds of
material, such as reprints of recent fiction. Two
main sequences: classified by Dewey number, and
alphabetical by author and title. There is also a
subject-index.

52   The National Union Catalogue of Monographs. A card
catalogue maintained at NLA, Canberra. 'NUCOM'.

NUCOM is a consolidated catalogue of the holdings of
monographs (i.e., books, not serials or most government publications) of all major Australian libraries.
It is thus the basic tool for locating books in
Australia. It contains an estimated over five
million cards representing over one million titles.
Publication on microfilm is forthcoming 1976. There
is a Guide to the National Union Catalogue of
Australia (3rd edn, Canberra, 1975), which includes
details of other union-lists such as SALSSAH (81),
but it is written primarily for librarians.

53   THE MITCHELL LIBRARY. Dictionary Catalog of Printed
Books. 38 vols. Hall, Boston, 1968. First
Supplement, 1970.

Catalogues the world's largest collection of
Australiana. Although primarily a listing of monographs, also includes many very useful analytical
subject-entries and periodical articles as well as
books. Although most notable for Australiana,
neither the library nor this catalogue is limited
to material of Australian interest.

54   FERGUSON, JOHN ALEXANDER. Bibliography of Australia.
7 vols. A & R, Sydney, 1941-69. Facsimile reprint,
NLA, Canberra, 1975- ; vols 1 & 2 published (with
supplementary locations list).

A full and detailed bibliography, with locations
for each item. In two parts: a chronological list
of Australiana, 1785-1850 (4 vols); and a list of
more restricted scope, arranged alphabetically by
author, 1851-1900 (3 vols). Literature is excluded
after 1850. Three volumes of addenda and an index
for 1851-1900 are in preparation. Some of the
limitations of Ferguson are discussed by Brian
McMullen in his review of the facsimile reprint,
Australian Library Journal, vol. 25, no. 1, February
1976, pp. 39-40).

55   Australian National Bibliography. NLA, Canberra,
      1961- . Weekly; monthly, four-monthly, and annual
      cumulations. Preceded by the Annual Catalogue of
      Australian Publications, 1937-61. 'ANB'.

      Lists books published in Australia, and overseas
      books of Australian interest. Currently arranged in
      a classified subject-sequence, with indexes to
      authors, titles, series, and subjects; arrangement
      has varied.

56   Australian Government Publications. NLA, Canberra,
      1952- . Quarterly; annual cumulation.

      The publications of each government (federal and
      state) are classified by subject; there is also an
      index of subjects. Most government publications are
      now included in the ANB (55), but the exact relation-
      ship between the two works has varied.

57   Index Translationum : Répertoire international des
      traductions / International Bibliography of
      Translations. Unesco, Paris, 1949- . Annual.
      Cumulative Index 1948-1968, 2 vols, Hall, Boston,
      1973.

      Limited to separately-published translations.
      Arranged by country of publication with no attempt
      to separate different languages used in the same
      country or to bring together all translations into
      a particular language. Each entry includes the
      work's title in its original language, and there is
      an author index in each volume. The Cumulative
      Index, however, is not entirely reliable. An earlier
      series was published under the same title (31
      quarterly numbers; Paris, 1932-40).

ii   Manuscripts

      A particular manuscript is much less easy to locate
than a particular book, especially if it has found its way
to an unexpected place, or if its existence or survival is
uncertain. One must often rely on general descriptive
guides to collections of manuscripts; few libraries have
published detailed catalogues. An exception is the
Mitchell Library (293). Many of the most important
collections of Australian literary manuscripts in Australian
libraries are listed in Chapter V.

      It is in the use of unpublished manuscript sources
that researchers most often encounter difficulties with
copyright. Collections of correspondence are especially
likely to present problems. They are frequently given to
a library by the recipient, yet copyright remains with the
writer of the letters. A valuable discussion of the
potential difficulties involved in the use of such material
is Michael Saclier, 'Archivists, Users, and the Copyright

Act, 1968', Archives and Manuscripts, vol. 6, no. 3, May
1975, pp. 72-86. The Copyright Act 1968 is the basis of
Australian copyright law. The standard legal textbook on
the subject is Copinger and Skone James on Copyright (11th
edn, London, 1971). More immediately useful and accessible
is Geoffrey Sawer, A Guide to Australian Law for Journal-
ists, Authors, Printers and Publishers (2nd edn, Melbourne,
1968). Sawer's discussion of copyright takes account of
the 1968 act.

58   THORPE, JAMES. The Use of Manuscripts in Literary
      Research : Problems of Access and Literary Property
      Rights. Modern Language Association of America,
      New York, 1974.

      Sound advice on the many problems involved in
      working with manuscripts. The author is director
      of the Huntington Library, California, one of the
      most important repositories of manuscripts in the
      United States.

59   Guide to Collections of Manuscripts Relating to
      Australia. NLA, Canberra, 1965- . Issued in
      loose-leaf instalments of 300 pages. Each instal-
      ment (11 published to date) is indexed, with a
      cumulative index to each group of four.

      Entries (limited to a single page) describe rather
      than catalogue the collections, and indicate the
      terms on which they may be used. The size and
      importance of the collections vary greatly, as does
      the detail in which they are described. All the
      collections are in Australia.

60   MANDER-JONES, PHYLLIS. Manuscripts in the British
      Isles Relating to Australia, New Zealand and the
      Pacific. Australian National University Press,
      Canberra, 1972.

      Describes individual manuscripts, but the detail
      naturally varies with their importance. The arrange-
      ment is geographical by repository, but there is an
      index of authors and subjects.

61   The National Union Catalog of Manuscript Collections.
      Library of Congress, Washington, 1959- . Annual.

      Very brief summary guides to collections of manu-
      scripts (on all subjects) in American libraries.
      The entries are arranged in no particular sequence,
      but there is an index of subject-strengths in each
      issue, and these indexes are partially cumulated.

iii   Theses

      At least one copy of a postgraduate thesis will usually
be kept by the institution that awarded the degree for which
it was written. Serial bibliographies are published of
higher-degree theses accepted by Australian, British, and

American universities (among others). All three are
seriously in arrears, making it difficult to locate theses
accepted recently. In the United States, doctoral theses
are published on microfilm almost as a matter of course.

62   Union List of Higher Degree Theses in Australian
      University Libraries : Cumulative Edition to 1965.
      University of Tasmania Library, Hobart, 1967.
      Supplement, 1966-1968, 1971; Supplement, 1969-1971,
      1974.

      Arranged by subject-area, with an index of authors.
      Seriously in arrears; supplements for 1972-73 and
      1974 have been announced for 1976. More up-to-date
      is ANU's list of Theses Accepted for Higher Degrees
      (new edn, Canberra, 1975; annual supplements
      planned). Many theses in progress (not always
      identified as such) are recorded in 'Research in
      Progress' in ALS (269).

63   Index to Theses Accepted for Higher Degrees by the
      Universities of Great Britain and Ireland and the
      Council for National Academic Awards. ASLIB, London,
      1953 (for 1950-51)- . Annual.

      Arranged by subject, with an author-index. Usually
      published about two years in arrears.

64   Comprehensive Dissertation Index, 1861-1972. 37 vols.
      Xerox University Microfilms, Ann Arbor, 1973.
      Annual. Supplements, 1974- .

      The main sequence indexes about 417,000 theses;
      'comprehensive' only for theses accepted by American
      universities. Within broad subject-areas (e.g.
      'Language and Literature') theses are indexed under
      all the keywords in their title; thus a thesis with
      a misleading title may be missed. There is also an
      author-index. Includes doctoral theses only.

65   Dissertation Abstracts International. Xerox
      University Microfilms, Ann Arbor, 1952- . Monthly;
      since 1966 in 2 series (Series A, 'The Humanities
      and Social Sciences'). 'DAI'.

      Not simply a list of theses, but a collection of
      abstracts, each written by the author of the thesis.
      Includes doctoral theses only. Each issue is
      classified under subject-areas, with indexes to
      authors and keywords. Also indexed in Comprehensive
      Dissertation Index (64). Microfilm or xerox copies
      of almost all theses abstracted can be ordered from
      University Microfilms.

iv   *Essays, articles, and reviews.*

Essays, articles, and reviews are rarely entered
separately in library catalogues. Instead they must be
located through the various indexes to such material.
These indexes have many uses, both current and retrospective.
Serial indexes provide rapid access to contemporary sources,
often well in advance of bibliographies. In retrospect
their particular usefulness is that (within their defined
scope) they are not usually selective, including brief or
ephemeral items of the kind often excluded from reference
works. Both these functions are illustrated in the uses
to which book-review indexes are put: the latest issues
offer a sample opinion of recent books, before mature
testing and assessment is possible; while in retrospect
they become a record of contemporary reaction.

66   POOLE, WILLIAM FREDERICK & FLETCHER, WILLIAM I.
      Poole's Index to Periodical Literature, 1802-1881.
      New edn. 2 vols. Houghton, Boston, 1891. Five
      Supplements cover 1882-1906. 1st edn 1848.

      A very useful subject-index to the contents of a
      wide range of journals. Its usefulness is enhanced
      by two ancillary aids. Poole does not index authors
      as contributors, only authors as subjects; this
      deficiency is remedied by C. Edward Wall's
      Cumulative Author Index (Ann Arbor, 1971). Marion
      V. Bell & Jean C. Bacon, Poole's Index Date and
      Volume Key (Chicago, 1957), tabulates the periodicals
      indexed and makes it easier to identify Poole's
      often cryptic references.

67   CUSHING, HELEN GRANT & MORRIS, ADAH V. Nineteenth
      Century Readers' Guide to Periodical Literature,
      1890-1899. 2 vols. Wilson, New York, 1944.

      Less comprehensive, but often more useful, than
      Poole (66) for the period and the journals that it
      covers. Unlike Poole, it indexes authors as
      contributors. It also identifies the authors of
      many anonymous articles on the evidence of office
      files. Indexes fifty-one serious periodicals,
      mostly general and literary; fourteen are also
      indexed beyond 1899 to the year (1922 in one case)
      when they were first included in one of the other
      Wilson indexes.

68   HOUGHTON, WALTER E. & others (eds). The Wellesley
      Index to Victorian Periodicals, 1824-1900.
      University of Toronto Press, Toronto, 1966- . 2
      vols published.

      Gives an issue-by-issue list of contents (often
      identifying anonymous or pseudonymous contributors,
      citing its authorities for doing so) for each
      periodical treated. Index of contributors, but not

of subjects. For subject-indexes see Poole (66) and
Cushing & Morris (67).

69   Readers' Guide to Periodical Literature. Wilson, New
York, 1900- . Twice monthly (monthly in July and
August); annual cumulations.

Basically an author/subject-index to about 160
American popular magazines. Chiefly of interest
as a guide to American popular culture and the world
as seen by that culture.

70   Humanities Index. Wilson, New York, 1974-
Quarterly; annual cumulations.

Indexes about 260 periodicals, including the most
important American serious and academic journals.
Little overlap with British Humanities Index (71);
sparse coverage of non-American sources. Nominally
the successor of two earlier Wilson indexes:
International Index to Periodicals (1907-65) and
Social Sciences and Humanities Index (1966-74).
In fact neither of these covered the humanities
nearly so well as Humanities Index does.

71   British Humanities Index. Library Association,
London, 1963- . Quarterly; annual cumulations.
'BHI'.

Indexes about 380 serials (from learned journals
to popular magazines) on a wide range of subjects.
The British equivalent of the Readers' Guide (69)
and the Humanities Index (70). Comparable coverage
for 1915-22 and 1926-62 was provided by the Library
Association's Subject Index to Periodicals.

72   MITCHELL LIBRARY. Index to Periodicals. 5 vols.
Trustees of the Public Library of New South Wales,
Sydney, 1950-66.

Cumulates an index of Australiana published in the
library's Bulletin, where it was continued
(uncumulated) until June 1964. The cumulation covers
1944-59 in four vols; vol. 5 (1960-63) was called
Australian Periodical Index.

73   Essay and General Literature Index. Wilson, New
York, 1934 (for 1900-33)- . Quarterly; annual
cumulations. Larger cumulations for 1900-74.

Indexes composite volumes (such as collections of
essays) by author and subject, thus complementing
the indexes to periodicals. Especially useful for
articles published in unlikely or obscure books.
There is an index to the authors, editors, and
titles of the nearly ten thousand composite
volumes indexed before 1970: Essay and General
Literature Index : Works Indexed 1900-69 (New York,
1972).

74   Book Review Digest. Wilson, New York, 1905- .
      Monthly (except February and July); alternate
      issues cumulate the one before; annual cumulations,
      with five-yearly cumulative indexes. 'BRD'.

      The most selective index of reviews; but useful for
      its excerpts (often about 100 words) from the
      reviews indexed. Selects its reviews from about
      eighty journals, mostly semi-popular American ones,
      with a few British (e.g. TLS, Encounter). Arranged
      by author, with an index of titles and subjects. Its
      usefulness will be enhanced by the forthcoming
      Book Review Digest Author/Title Index 1905-1974.

75   Book Review Index. Gale, Detroit, 1965- . 6 times
      yearly; alternate issues cumulate the one before;
      annual cumulations. 'BRI'.

      Indexes (by author only) reviews in about 230
      journals, mostly American with a few Canadian and
      British. More comprehensive than BRD (74), but
      without excerpts.

76   An Index to Book Reviews in the Humanities. Thomson,
      Detroit, 1960- . Annual.

      The most useful source for serious study, indexing
      about 275 journals. Some overlap with BRI (75),
      but its narrower scope allows many more literary
      periodicals to be indexed. Includes several major
      Australian journals and many British ones. Each
      volume lists the issues of the journals it indexes;
      major gaps are noted, and where possible these are
      filled retrospectively.

77   The New York Times Index. New York Times, New York,
      1913- . Fortnightly; various intermediate
      cumulations; annual cumulations.

      A very thorough (and complex) analytical index.
      Its classified subject entries make it far more
      useful than The Times Index (78). Coverage has
      been retrospectively extended back to 1851 when
      the paper began publication. There is a separate
      cumulative index to obituaries (104).

78   The Times Index. Newspaper Archive Developments,
      Reading, 1906- . Quarterly; frequency has varied.

      Spartan compared to the New York Times Index (77);
      cumbersome to use because uncumulated. For the
      period 1790-1941 there is also Samuel Palmer's
      Index to 'The Times' Newspaper (London, 1868-1943).

79   Index to the Sydney Morning Herald and Sydney Mail.
      Fairfax, Sydney, 1927-61. Quarterly.

      Indexed the Sydney Morning Herald (1927-61); the
      Sydney Mail (1927-38); the Sunday Herald (1949-53);
      and the Sun-Herald (1953-61). Although publication

has ceased, an index is maintained at the paper's
office and is available to researchers. The
Melbourne Argus published an index 1910-49.

80   Australian Public Affairs Information Service : A
     Subject Index to Current Literature. NLA, Canberra,
     1945- . Monthly (except December); annual
     cumulations. 'APAIS'.

     Currently a subject-index to periodicals in the
     humanities and social sciences. Many journals are
     indexed comprehensively, whatever their content.
     All other Australian serials received by NLA are
     scanned for items of Australian interest. Also
     indexes feature-articles in major newspapers.
     APAIS has changed a great deal, and before using it
     as a retrospective index it is essential to check
     its scope at the time.

81   Serials in Australian Libraries : Social Sciences
     and Humanities. Rev. edn. 4 vols. NLA, Canberra,
     1968-74. Updated by Newly Reported Titles (monthly
     except December); these are cumulated in four-
     monthly Supplements, which are not confined to new
     titles. 'SALSSAH'.

82   Union List of Serials in the Libraries of the United
     States and Canada. 3rd edn. 5 vols. Wilson, New
     York, 1965. Supplemented by New Serial Titles
     1950-1970 (4 vols, Library of Congress, Washington,
     1973) and its serial continuation New Serial Titles
     (monthly; various cumulations).

83   British Union-Catalogue of Periodicals. 4 vols.
     Butterworth, London, 1955-58. Supplement to 1960,
     1962. New Periodical Titles, 1964- ; quarterly;
     annual cumulations; larger cumulatior for 1960-68.

     Three comparable works arranged in roughly the same
     way: serials are entered alphabetically with brief
     details of place, dates of publication, and the
     holdings of selected libraries. The more widely-
     held serials are reported selectively. The three
     vary in minor and annoying ways, especially in their
     entry rules. SALSSAH is obviously the most useful
     for Australian purposes, but many serials are not
     held in Australiar libraries and the others usefully
     supplement it.

84   Newspapers in Australian Libraries : A Union List.
     3rd edn. 2 parts. NLA, Canberra, 1973-75. 1st
     edn 1959-60.

     The standard source for locating newspaper holdings
     in Australia. Part 1 lists overseas newspapers;
     Part 2 Australian newspapers. The arrangement is by
     place of publication; there is also an index of
     titles. Precise dates for each library's holdings

are given (including microfilms). Many files held
in newspaper offices are recorded.

v   *Work in progress*

It is often useful and sometimes important to find
out about forthcoming publications and work in progress.
This task is both difficult and chancy. A useful, but far
from complete, listing of 'Research in Progress' is
published every two years in ALS (269). Each issue of
SPAN (288) also lists some work in progress. Authors
included in Contemporary Authors (133) often list details
of their current projects; many academic authors are
included. AULLA Newsletter (265) lists staff on study
leave, often with a very brief note of their research plans.

85   BINDOFF, S.T. & BOULTON, JAMES T. (eds). Research in
Progress in English and Historical Studies in the
Universities of the British Isles. St James Press,
London, 1971.

Compiled from questionnaires sent to academics;
projects are listed by subject with an author index.
A second edition (forthcoming 1976) will include
Australian literature as a subject and the research
projects of Australian academics.

86   Commonwealth Universities Yearbook. Association of
Commonwealth Universities, London, 1914- . Annual.

Not directly relevant, but useful for locating the
current addresses of scholars through the general
index of names. The entry for each university gives
the date at which the information was correct,
usually about the middle of the year before publication. More recent information can sometimes be
obtained from AUMLA (265), which publishes an annual
list of AULLA members; and from the AULLA Newsletter
(265), which records staff movements, not only those
of AULLA members.

II   OTHER REFERENCE SOURCES

This chapter includes the most useful sources of non-
bibliographical information likely to be needed in the
study of Australian literature: reference works for check-
ing facts, tracing allusions, and acquiring background
information on literary and other subjects.

A   Encyclopedias

87   The Encyclopaedia Britannica : A Dictionary of Arts,
      Sciences, Literature, and General Information. 11th
      edn. 29 vols. Cambridge University Press, Cambridge,
      1910-11. 1st edn 1768-71.

      This edition contains much humanistic learning
      omitted from later science-oriented editions.
      Virtually a summary of what the nineteenth century
      knew, it remains a scholarly landmark and a mine of
      miscellaneous information.

88   The New Encyclopaedia Britannica. 15th edn. 30 vols.
      Benton, Chicago, 1974.

      Arranged in three parts: Propaedia (1 vol.); Micro-
      paedia (10 vols); Macropaedia (19 vols). The Pro-
      paedia is an elaborate classification of subjects and
      sub-subjects; it could be useful in making a list
      of articles to consult on a subject not itself given
      an entry. The Micropaedia is a ready-reference work;
      its entries are short and explanatory. There are
      many cross-references to the longer articles in the
      Macropaedia, where topics of importance are given
      discursive treatment. Easier to use than it sounds;
      a good source of general information. There is an
      American bias in the selection and treatment of
      subjects.

89   HARRIS, WILLIAM H. & LEVEY, JUDITH S. (eds). The
      New Columbia Encyclopedia. Columbia University
      Press, New York, 1975. 1st edn 1935.

      A good one-volume source of general information.
      Individual articles tend to be longer than those in
      Britannica's Micropaedia but much shorter than those
      in the Macropaedia (88). For some topics Columbia
      has a single succinct entry assembling information
      scattered over several in Britannica.

90   CHISHOLM ALEC. H. (ed.). The Australian Encyclopaedia.
      10 vols. Grolier Society of Australia, Sydney, 1965.
      1st edn (2 vols) 1925-26.

      A good source of general information about all
      aspects of Australia and Australians. The 1965
      edition (based on that of 1958) was thoroughly
      revised in detail, but its general outlook still
      reflects the mid-fifties. The first edition
      contains much that was subsequently omitted, and is
      still worth consulting. A new edition is in pre-
      paration.

B   Dictionaries

91   MURRAY, SIR JAMES & others (eds). The Oxford English
      Dictionary. Corrected reissue with supplement and
      bibliography. 13 vols. Clarendon Press, Oxford,
      1933. 1st edn 1885-1928. 'OED'.

      The standard English dictionary on historical
      principles; copious quotations illustrate the
      history of every word.

92   BURCHFIELD, R.W. (ed.). A Supplement to the Oxford
      English Dictionary. 4 vols. Clarendon Press,
      Oxford, 1972- . Vol. 1 (A-G) published, vol. 2
      (H-N) forthcoming 1976.

      Not confined to the period since the OED (91) was
      published; frequently supplements it for earlier
      usage.

93   LITTLE, H.W. & others (eds). The Shorter Oxford
      English Dictionary on Historical Principles. 3rd
      edn, with rev. etymologies. 2 vols. Clarendon
      Press, Oxford, 1973. 1st edn 1933; 3rd edn 1944.

      A condensed version of the OED (91), retaining its
      principle of illustrative quotation on a smaller
      scale. In the 1973 revision the etymologies reflect
      recent research, and there is an enlarged supplement
      of recent words and usages.

94   FOWLER, F.G. & H.W. The Pocket Oxford Dictionary of
      Current English. 5th edn, rev. E. McIntosh.
      Clarendon Press, Oxford, 1969. 1st edn 1924.

      A handy desk-dictionary limited to current usage.
      The 1969 edition has a 'Supplement of Australian and
      New Zealand Words' by R.W. Burchfield. Current
      English is treated on a larger scale in the Concise
      Oxford Dictionary (6th edn, forthcoming 1976),
      although without any special Australian content. An
      Australian Pocket Oxford Dictionary, edited by
      Grahame Johnston (forthcoming 1976), will be a

complete revision of the Pocket Oxford Dictionary
for Australian use with all specifically Australian
words and usages incorporated in the body of the
dictionary.

95   MORRIS, EDWARD E. Austral English : A Dictionary of
Australasian Words, Phrases, and Usages. Macmillan,
London, 1898. Several facsimile reprints: one
(Sydney University Press, Sydney, 1972) has a fore-
word by H.L. Rogers.

Includes only specifically Australasian words and
usages; illustrated with precisely-identified
quotations. Very useful for its period; there is
no comparable work for more recent usages. For
other works on Australian English, see Blair (29).

96   GOVE, PHILIP BABCOCK (ed.). Webster's Third New
International Dictionary of the English Language.
Merriam, Springfield, 1961. 1st edn 1909.

The standard American dictionary. This third
edition abandoned the prescriptive functions of its
predecessors and met with a mixed reception.
Provides the most comprehensive account of how
English is used in the United States. Coverage of
Australian English is also good, especially for
plants, animals and fishes.

97   MORRIS, WILLIAM (ed.). The American Heritage
Dictionary of the English Language. American
Heritage, Boston, 1969. Later reprints incorporate
minor revisions and updatings.

Although much smaller than Webster's (96), American
Heritage does set out to provide guidance about
correct usages. American Heritage's superior typo-
graphy makes it easier to consult, and it naturally
includes more recent coinages.

98   BARNHART, CLARENCE L. & others. The Barnhart
Dictionary of New English since 1963. Barnhart,
Bronxville, 1973.

A good source for neologisms; illustrated by
precisely-identified quotations, often from a
specialized source.

99   FARMER, JOHN & HENLEY, W.E. Slang and Its Analogues,
Past and Present. 7 vols. Privately printed,
London, 1890-1904. Rev. edn of vol. 1 (in 2 vols)
1903-09.

A good scholarly source, illustrating usages with
precisely-identified quotations.

100 PARTRIDGE, ERIC. A Dictionary of Slang and Uncon-
ventional English. 7th edn. 2 vols. Routledge,
London, 1970. 1st edn 1937.

Less scholarly than Farmer & Henley (99); few
precise references. Material added since the first
edition is in vol. 2. Coverage of Australian slang
is good; Partridge was educated in Australia.

C Biographical dictionaries

i General

101 SLOCUM, ROBERT B. Biographical Dictionaries and
Related Works. Gale, Detroit, 1967. Supplement,
1972.

A classified bibliography of biographical dictionaries; indexes of authors, titles, and subjects.
The Supplement is almost as large as the main volume,
and is not confined to more recent works.

102 Webster's Biographical Dictionary. New edn. Merriam,
Springfield, 1972. 1st edn 1943.

The most comprehensive general-purpose biographical
dictionary, with about 40,000 entries. The typical
entry is about eighty words, giving a factual
career-summary. Treatment of recent figures and
events is uneven; successive editions since 1943
have been partial revisions, not total rewritings.
No bibliographical references. Generally superior
to Chambers's Biographical Dictionary (rev. edn,
Edinburgh, 1974) which occasionally supplements it.

103 HYAMSON, ALBERT M. A Dictionary of Universal
Biography of All Ages and of All Peoples. 2nd edn.
Routledge, London, 1951. 1st edn 1916.

One-line entries give name, dates, occupation or
notability, and a reference to a standard source
such as a national biographical dictionary.
Contains about 55,000 entries. Actually a more
useful supplement to Webster's (102) than this
figure suggests, since Hyamson is stronger on the
non-English-speaking world and on minor figures
before 1900.

104 The New York Times Obituaries Index, 1858-1968.
New York Times, New York, 1970.

About 117,000 entries, indexing a very useful source
for both major and minor figures.

105 Biography Index : A Cumulative Index to Biographical Material in Books and Magazines. Wilson, New York, 1946- . Quarterly; annual cumulations. Larger cumulations for 1946-73.

Useful for locating recent material, and in retrospect for brief, ephemeral, and popular items. Like the other Wilson indexes, it draws on predominantly American sources.

ii   British

106 STEPHEN, LESLIE & LEE, SIDNEY (eds). Dictionary of National Biography. 63 vols. Smith Elder, London, 1885-1900. Supplement, 3 vols, 1901. Reprinted (including Supplement) in 22 vols, 1908-09. Second Supplement (covering 1901-11), 3 vols, 1912. Five further supplements (covering 1912-60) by various editors have been published (OUP, London, 1927-71). 'DNB'.

The standard source for British biography, including notable colonials. The main sequence and its Supplement include people who died on or before 22 January 1901 (the death of Queen Victoria). The twentieth-century supplements, each covering a decade, include a cumulative index to post-1900 entries. There is a volume of Corrections and Additions (Boston, 1966).

107 The Dictionary of National Biography : The Concise Dictionary. 2 vols. OUP, London, 1953-61. 1st edn 1903. 'Concise DNB'.

Originally published as an index and epitome of the DNB (106); abstracts every entry in the parent work. An important appendix of corrections was added to the 1953 reprint.

108 Who's Who. Black, London, 1897- . Annual.

Factual career-summaries, based on information supplied by the subject. Predominantly but not exclusively British in scope. Final entries (1897-1970) are cumulated in Who Was Who (6 vols, London, 1920-72).

iii   Australian

109 ARNOLD, JOHN. 'What's What in Who's Who'. Australian Studies Booklist, no. 1, 1974, pp. 1-11. 'Addenda', no. 2, 1974-75, pp. 28-30.

A general survey of Australian biographical sources with an extensive bibliography. A much fuller Australian listing than Slocum (101); not confined to formal biographical dictionaries.

110   <u>Biographical Register Short List</u>. New edn. 2 vols.
       Department of History, Australian National University,
       Canberra, 1963. 1st edn 1959.

       An index of Australian biography on the same plan as
       Hyamson (103). Includes references to many newspaper
       obituaries.

111   PIKE, DOUGLAS (ed.). <u>Australian Dictionary of</u>
       <u>Biography</u>. Melbourne University Press, Melbourne,
       1966- . 5 vols published: 1788-1850, 2 vols;
       1851-1890 (A-Q) 3 vols; 1851-1890 (R-Z) forthcoming
       1976. '<u>ADB</u>'.

       When completed will be the standard biographical
       source for people who made their main contribution
       to Australian history before 1938. The current
       general editors are Bede Nairn and A.G. Serle. The
       <u>ADB</u> Unit (Research School of Social Sciences,
       Australian National University, Canberra) acts as a
       clearing-house for Australian biographical inform-
       ation, whether or not it falls within the scope of
       the <u>ADB</u>.

112   SERLE, PERCIVAL. <u>Dictionary of Australian Biography</u>.
       2 vols. A & R, Sydney, 1949.

       Includes men (and a few women) who died before the
       end of 1942. Even when the <u>ADB</u> (111) is completed,
       Serle's work will continue to provide a valuable
       historical perspective.

113   LEGGE, J.S. (ed.). <u>Who's Who in Australia</u>. Herald
       & Weekly Times, Melbourne, 1906- . Triennial.

       Factual career-summaries based on information
       supplied by the subject. The older editions remain
       useful for minor figures. It can also be rewarding
       to trace a subject's entry through several success-
       ive editions. Originally edited by Fred Johns, the
       work has changed its title several times: <u>Johns's</u>
       <u>Notable Australians</u> (1906-08); <u>Fred Johns's Annual</u>
       (1912-14); <u>Who's Who in the Commonwealth of</u>
       <u>Australia</u> (1922); <u>Who's Who in Australia</u> (1927-).

D   <u>Literature</u>

                    i   General works

114   BENET, WILLIAM ROSE. <u>The Reader's Encyclopedia</u>.
       2nd edn. Crowell, New York, 1965. 1st edn 1948.

       A good quick-reference source for literary and
       miscellaneous information: entries for important
       individual works, characters, places, allusions,

and major historical figures. For authors and
literary movements, fuller information will often
be found in Steinberg (115) or the Penguin
Companion (116).

115   STEINBERG, S.H. (ed.). Cassell's Encyclopedia of
       World Literature. 2nd edn, rev. J. Buchanan-Brown.
       3 vols. Cassell, London, 1973. 1st edn 1953.

116   DAICHES, DAVID & others. (eds). The Penguin
       Companion to Literature. 4 vols. Penguin, Harmonds-
       worth, 1969-71. vol. 1, Britain and the Common-
       wealth; vol. 2, European; vol. 3, U.S.A., Latin
       America; vol. 4, Classical, Byzantine, Oriental,
       African.

       Two useful reference works of about the same scope.
       Steinberg divides general articles (vol. 1) from
       author biographies (vols 2 & 3). Penguin has a
       single sequence for each of its eight geographical
       areas. Steinberg has longer general articles on
       many subjects, especially on topics which cut across
       the Penguin boundaries. Penguin has longer author
       entries, more ambitiously critical and less confined
       to facts than Steinberg's. Yet Steinberg includes
       many authors who are not in Penguin, while there are
       very few of whom the reverse is true. Steinberg
       also has fuller and more up-to-date bibliographical
       information. Both are liable to small slips
       (especially with dates).

117   GREEN, H.M. A History of Australian Literature :
       Pure and Applied. 2 vols. A & R, Sydney, 1961.
       Reprinted with corrections, 1966.

       Written over a long period, and therefore less
       modern than its date would suggest. Nevertheless
       an indispensable work of reference, inclusive and
       well-organized. General discussions of genres and
       periods are followed by bibliographical and critical
       accounts of a large number of individual authors.
       Also useful discussions of newspapers, periodicals,
       and non-fiction.

ii   Literary terms

118   ABRAMS, M.H. A Glossary of Literary Terms. 3rd edn.
       Holt, New York, 1971. 1st edn 1941.

       Good explanatory articles, with selective reading-
       lists. For the less common rhetorical terms consult
       the OED (91); for terms connected with poetry or
       poetics, see also Preminger (124).

119   SHIPLEY, JOSEPH T. (ed.).   Dictionary of World
       Literary Terms : Forms, Techniques, Criticism.   3rd
       edn. Allen & Unwin, London, 1970. 1st edn 1943.

       The dictionary of terms occupies the greater part of
       the book; there are also longer articles on
       literary criticism in many important countries, and
       brief lists of important critics from other countries.
       There is a list of contributors, but individual
       articles are not signed.

120   FOWLER, ROGER (ed.). A Dictionary of Modern Critical
       Terms. Routledge, London, 1973.

       More argumentative and less purely informative than
       Abrams (118) or Shipley (119). As a result often
       more stimulating, and occasionally infuriating. The
       standard varies; the great majority of the articles
       are written by Fowler's colleagues at the University
       of East Anglia. There is a discernible bias towards
       rhetorical rather than historical criticism. Not
       the book to consult first.

           iii   Dictionaries of quotations

121   STEVENSON, BURTON. Stevenson's Book of Quotations,
       Classical and Modern. 10th edn. Cassell, London,
       1967. 1st edn 1934.

122   BARTLETT, JOHN. Familiar Quotations : A Collection
       of Phrases and Proverbs Traced to Their Sources in
       Ancient and Modern Literature. 14th edn, rev. E.M.
       Beck. Little Brown, Boston, 1968. 1st edn 1855.

123   Oxford Dictionary of Quotations. 2nd edn. OUP,
       London, 1953. 1st edn 1941.

       Each has its particular strengths and weaknesses.
       Stevenson is organized by subject, the other two by
       author. Stevenson has about 70,000 entries;
       Bartlett, 45,000; and Oxford about 20,000. A new
       edition of Oxford is in preparation.

           iv   Genre handbooks

124   PREMINGER, ALEXANDER S. & others (eds). Princeton
       Encyclopedia of Poetry and Poetics. Enlarged edn.
       Macmillan, London, 1975. 1st edn 1965.

       Signed articles of varying lengths on poetics and
       the history, techniques, and literary relations of
       poetry. No entries for individual poets or poems.
       The new material in the enlarged edition is confined
       to a supplement.

125   McGraw-Hill Encyclopedia of World Drama. 4 vols.
       McGraw-Hill, New York, 1972.

       Emphasis on drama as literature rather than as a
       performing art; most of the entries are for authors
       The usefulness of the numerous illustrations is
       impaired by inadequate captioning.

126   GASSNER, JOHN & QUINN, EDWARD. The Reader's
       Encyclopedia of World Drama. Crowell, New York,
       1969.

       On individual authors McGraw-Hill (125) is fuller,
       but Gassner & Quinn has general articles on many
       topics not treated in McGraw-Hill.

127   REES, LESLIE. The Making of Australian Drama : A
       Historical and Critical Survey from the 1830s to
       the 1970s. A & R, Sydney, 1973.

       The best descriptive history of Australian drama,
       a revised and expanded version of Rees's Towards
       an Australian Drama (Sydney, 1953). Has a selective
       bibliography and extensive checklists of plays
       published since 1936 or broadcast on ABC radio or
       television. See also (22-24).

128   BAKER, ERNEST A. & PACKMAN, JAMES. A Guide to the
       Best Fiction, English and American, Including
       Translations from Foreign Languages. Enlarged edn.
       Macmillan, New York, 1932. 1st edn 1903.

       Brief synopses; indexes titles, major subjects,
       themes, and characters. Particularly useful for
       its coverage of minor nineteenth-century novelists.

129   SAXBY, H.M. A History of Australian Children's
       Literature 1841-1941; A History of Australian
       Children's Literature 1941-1970, with supplementary
       chapters by Marjorie Cotton. Wentworth Press,
       Sydney, 1969-71.

       The standard account, often prescriptive and
       moralistic. Contains a chronological bibliography;
       for an author bibliography see Muir (27). See also
       Australian Book Review (267).

          v   Twentieth-century literature

130   FLEISCHMANN, BERNARD (ed.). Encyclopedia of World
       Literature in the Twentieth Century. 3 vols.
       Ungar, New York, 1969-71.

       Basically an author-dictionary with some general
       articles on national literatures and literary
       movements. Articles (each with bibliography) are
       generous in length, offering critical appraisals as
       well as career-outlines. Much of the material is
       translated and updated from the Herder Lexikon der
       Weltliteratur im 20. Jahrhundert (2 vols, Freiburg,
       1960-61).

131   KUNITZ, STANLEY J. & HAYCRAFT, HOWARD. <u>Twentieth</u>
       <u>Century Authors : A Biographical Dictionary of</u>
       <u>Modern Literature</u>. Wilson, New York, 1942. <u>First</u>
       <u>Supplement</u>, 1955.

       Biographies of about 1,850 authors who flourished
       after 1900 and who achieved some reputation in the
       English-speaking world. Many living authors con-
       tributed sketches for their own entries; these are
       clearly separated from editorial comment. The
       <u>Supplement</u> is not confined to additional authors but
       includes supplementary entries for many already
       treated in the main volume.

132   WAKEMAN, JOHN (ed.). <u>World Authors 1950-1970</u>.
       Wilson, New York, 1975.

       Compiled on the same plan as <u>Twentieth Century</u>
       <u>Authors</u> (131). Includes about 950 authors who have
       achieved recognition since about 1950; approximately
       half contributed autobiographical sketches.

133   ETHRIDGE, JAMES M. & others (eds). <u>Contemporary</u>
       <u>Authors : A Biobibliographical Guide to Current</u>
       <u>Authors and Their Works</u>. Gale, Detroit, 1962- .
       Irregular.

       Not confined to 'creative writers'; good coverage
       of academic and general non-fiction writers.
       Entries are based on information supplied by the
       subject; many list work in progress. Some earlier
       volumes were published in revised editions; there
       is now a <u>Permanent Series</u> (1975-) for final
       entries. Cumulative indexes to all entries are
       published periodically.

134   VINSON, JAMES (ed.). <u>Contemporary Poets</u>. 2nd edn.
       St James Press, London, 1975. 1st edn 1970.

135   VINSON, JAMES (ed.). <u>Contemporary Novelists</u>. St
       James Press, London, 1972.

136   VINSON, JAMES (ed.). <u>Contemporary Dramatists</u>. St
       James Press, London, 1972.

       Three complementary volumes; confined to writers
       in English. Author-entries may contain a brief
       biography, a list of published works, a selective
       bibliography, an independent critical appraisal,
       and material supplied by the subject. <u>Contemporary</u>
       <u>Novelists</u> (2nd edn forthcoming 1976) includes
       writers of short fiction. Coverage of Australian
       authors is comprehensive in <u>Contemporary Poets</u>,
       adequate in <u>Contemporary Novelists</u>, minimal in
       <u>Contemporary Dramatists</u>. For many minor authors
       these volumes may provide the only reference source.

E   Ancillary subjects

i   History

137   LANGER, WILLIAM L. Encyclopedia of World History
      Ancient, Medieval, and Modern, Chronologically
      Arranged. 5th edn. Houghton, Boston, 1972. 1st
      edn 1940.

      A conspectus of events arranged by area and date;
      useful for checking the precise date of any event.
      Index of proper names.

138   HOWAT, G.M.D. (ed.). Dictionary of World History.
      Nelson, London, 1973.

      Entries for people, places, events, political
      parties, general topics.

139   CROWLEY, F.K. (ed.). A New History of Australia.
      Heinemann, Melbourne, 1974.

      Individual chapters by different authors cover
      periods of between ten and twenty years;
      extensive bibliography divided into the same
      periods.

ii   Folklore

140   LEACH, MARIA (ed.). Funk and Wagnall's Standard
      Dictionary of Folklore, Mythology, and Legend.
      Rev. edn. Funk & Wagnall, New York, 1972. 1st
      edn 1950.

141   JOBES, GERTRUDE. Dictionary of Mythology, Folklore,
      and Symbols. 2 vols. Scarecrow Press, New York,
      1961.

      Leach has longer and fuller articles, but Jobes has
      many brief explanatory entries for names and symbols
      not treated individually in Leach. Leach has
      bibliographical references; Jobes not. The revised
      edition of Leach is corrected rather than fully up-
      dated but a useful index is added.

142   Brewer's Dictionary of Phrase and Fable. Centenary
      edn, rev. Ivor H. Evans. Cassell, London, 1970.
      1st edn 1870.

      Useful for tracing allusions and for explanations
      of 'words that tell a story'; contains much
      miscellaneous information about proper names. The
      1952 edition is also worth consulting for material
      subsequently omitted.

143   The Oxford Dictionary of English Proverbs. 3rd edn,
       rev. F.P. Wilson. Clarendon Press, Oxford, 1970.
       1st edn 1935.

       Gives the earliest recorded uses of proverbs; also
       useful for checking phrases and allusions suspected
       to be quotations or proverbs, for which see also
       the dictionaries of quotations (121-23).

144   FEARN-WANNAN, W. Australian Folklore : A Dictionary
       of Lore, Legends, and Popular Allusions. Lansdowne,
       Melbourne, 1970.

       An Australian 'folk treasury': an alphabetical
       sequence of the folk stories behind popular express-
       ions, legends, phrases, and superstitions. Also
       includes events, characters, and places that have
       passed into popular mythology.

                    iii   The arts

145   SERLE, GEOFFREY. From Deserts the Prophets Come :
       The Creative Spirit in Australia 1788-1972.
       Heinemann, Melbourne, 1973.

       A discursive history of Australian culture; largely
       a synthesis of existing histories in various fields,
       but an interesting one. The notes and bibliography
       provide a useful guide to further reading.

146   Encyclopedia of World Art. 15 vols. McGraw-Hill,
       New York, 1959-68.

       The standard reference source on the plastic arts;
       copiously illustrated with about 500 pages of plates
       in each volume.

147   McCULLOCH, ALAN. Encyclopedia of Australian Art.
       Hutchinson, Richmond, 1968.

       Not an encyclopedia: a skeleton dictionary of
       artists, galleries, etc. Marred by inaccuracies
       and lack of adequate documentation. More can often
       be learned from Bernard Smith's narratives (148-49).

148   SMITH, BERNARD. European Vision and the South
       Pacific 1768-1850 : A Study in the History of
       Art and Ideas. Clarendon Press, Oxford, 1960.

149   SMITH, BERNARD. Australian Painting 1788-1970.
       2nd edn. OUP, Melbourne, 1971. 1st edn 1962.

       Both are critical studies rather than reference
       works, but their extensive documentation and
       illustration give them status as such. Both are
       more reliable than McCulloch (147).

150   Grove's Dictionary of Music and Musicians. 5th edn,
        ed. Eric Blom. 9 vols. Macmillan, London, 1954.
        Supplementary Volume, 1961. 1st edn 1878-89.

        The standard reference source in the English
        language. An entirely new edition (edited by
        Stanley Sadie) is in preparation.

151   APEL, WILLI (ed.). Harvard Dictionary of Music.
        2nd edn. Harvard University Press, Cambridge,
        1969: 1st edn 1944.

        A good quick-reference source, superior to the
        Oxford Companion to Music (10th edn, London, 1970)
        except for composers.

152   COVELL, ROGER. Australia's Music : Themes of a New
        Society. Sun Books, Melbourne, 1967.

        Combines historical narrative and critical assess-
        ment; references but no bibliography. Includes a
        discography of recorded Australian music.

III   AUTHORS

This chapter describes the most useful reference
sources for research on a particular author. They will
usually need to be supplemented by the general reference
works listed elsewhere in this book.

Australian literature and Australian authors have not
yet been adequately documented. Apart from the pioneering
bibliographies of Miller (1) and Macartney (2) and a few
notable author-bibliographies, most of the works in the field
are limited in scope and often unreliable and inaccurate.
For many authors no substantial work of reference exists.
Often there are only the selective checklists in introductory
studies such as Australian Writers and Their Work and
Twayne's World Authors Series. Although useful they are too
brief to be more than starting points. For many authors
omitted it is often worth consulting Contemporary Poets
(134), Contemporary Novelists (135) and Contemporary
Dramatists (136).

There are very few scholarly editions of Australian
authors, yet there are several whose works deserve good
editions. The texts of at least two important poets,
Harpur and Neilson, remain to be established. We hope that
the list of reference sources in this chapter, by drawing
attention to such deficiencies, will stimulate further
research.

This chapter includes textual, biographical, and
bibliographical studies and checklists. All of the bibliographies listed will need to be updated through the serial
bibliographies (5-10). Autobiographical works, interviews,
undocumented biographies and critical books and articles
are not listed here: they are accessible through one or
other of the reference works described or through the
general sources listed in Chapter I.

Books in five uniform series recur in this chapter
and their general features are described here to avoid
undue repetition.

1   Australian Writers and Their Work (AWW), published by
OUP (by Lansdowne until 1966), is a series of introductory
booklets usually on a single author, with a short biographical account, a critical study, and a select bibliography. Where there is no recent biography the first part
of an AWW may be useful. The bibliographies usually
include all an author's books (though seldom listing more
than first editions), other important publications, and a
selected list of secondary works.

2   Twayne's World Authors Series (TWAS) are introductory

biographical and critical guides on a larger scale than AWW
but differing in three respects: they contain a chronology;
they are indexed; and most importantly they have a longer,
annotated, bibliography.

3   Bibliographies of Australian Authors, formerly published
by the Libraries Board of South Australia, have been discon-
tinued, but are still updated in Supplements to the annual
cumulation of Index to Australian Book Reviews (7). These
classified checklists list an author's books, other publications (articles, poems, stories etc. in a single sequence),
biographical articles, critical articles and reviews (with
an inconsistent division into 'brief notices' and 'full
reviews'), photographs and illustrations, and miscellaneous
items. Photographs are listed (and numbered) separately
from the articles they accompany. The checklists appear to
have been compiled largely from secondary sources. Most
were severely reviewed but since they are more comprehensive
than AWW and TWAS they can, if used with caution, be useful
starting points.

4   Studies in Australian Bibliography usually offer more
detailed bibliographical descriptions than any of the
others. This series also contains five catalogues by Harry
F. Chaplin describing his collections of Brennan (160),
Lawson (204), Lindsay (207), McCrae (211) and Neilson (218).
These contain much unique material and the annotations
often give lengthy quotations from letters and manuscripts.

5   The Fryer Memorial Library of Australian Literature,
University of Queensland (300) issues many checklists in
typescript form. These are generally both thorough and
dependable, and are often more useful than published sources.
They are available from the Library for the cost of photo-
copying.

'Rolf Boldrewood'

(Thomas Alexander Browne, 1826-1915)

153   BURKE, KEAST. Thomas Alexander Browne (Rolf Boldre-
wood) : An Annotated Bibliography, Checklist and
Chronology. Studies in Australian Bibliography.
Stone, Cremorne, 1956.

Lists primary and secondary material, including some
manuscripts. Records serial publication of novels,
and notes content of poems, stories, and articles.

154   BRISSENDEN, ALAN. Rolf Boldrewood. AWW. OUP,
Melbourne, 1972.

Longer biography than usual in the series. Bibliography includes details of serial publications.
Supplements Burke (153) for more recent material.

Martin Boyd, 1893-1972

155   NASE, PAMELA. 'Martin Boyd : A Checklist'. <u>ALS</u>,
       vol. 5, no. 4, October 1972, pp. 404-14.

       A comprehensive list of Boyd's works (including
       translations) to 1970; brief descriptions of
       manuscript collections; lists of critical articles
       and reviews. Will be superseded by Brenda Niall's
       <u>Martin Boyd</u> (Australian Bibliographies, OUP,
       Melbourne, forthcoming 1976).

156   NIALL, BRENDA. <u>Martin Boyd</u>. AWW. OUP, Melbourne,
       1974.

       Includes a discussion of <u>The Montforts</u> revisions;
       the select bibliography supplements Nase (155) in
       some details. For a discussion of Boyd's revisions
       of the Langton novels see Niall, <u>ALS</u>, vol. 7, no. 3,
       May 1976, pp. 321-24.

       Christopher Brennan, 1870-1932

157   BRENNAN, CHRISTOPHER. <u>The Verse</u>. Eds A.R. Chisholm
       & J.J. Quinn. A & R, Sydney, 1960.

158   BRENNAN, CHRISTOPHER. <u>The Prose</u>. Eds A.R. Chisholm
       & J.J. Quinn. A & R, Sydney, 1962.

       Complete texts (omitting only some articles on
       classical literature) with textual notes.

159   STONE, WALTER W. & ANDERSON, HUGH. <u>Christopher
       Brennan : A Comprehensive Bibliography with
       Annotations</u>. Studies in Australian Bibliography.
       Stone, Cremorne, 1959.

       Bibliographical descriptions of Brennan's books;
       checklist of his other publications (including his
       translations); extensive annotated list of critical
       and biographical material. Though less compre-
       hensive, G.A. Wilkes, 'Writings of C.J. Brennan : a
       Checklist', <u>Meanjin</u>, vol. 15, no. 2, June 1956, pp.
       186-95, is useful and more accessible.

160   CHAPLIN, HARRY F. <u>A Brennan Collection : An Annotated
       Catalogue of First Editions, Inscribed Copies, Manu-
       scripts and Association Items</u>. Studies in Australian
       Bibliography. Wentworth Press, Sydney, 1966.

       Ninety-seven entries with extensive annotation and
       quotation.

161   McAULEY, JAMES. <u>Christopher Brennan</u>. AWW. 2nd edn.
       OUP, Melbourne, 1973. 1st edn 1963.

       The bibliography usefully supplements Stone &
       Anderson (159) for recent·criticism.

Marcus Clarke, 1846-81

162   CLARKE, MARCUS. <u>A Colonial City, High and Low Life</u> :
      <u>Selected Journalism of Marcus Clarke</u>. Ed. L.T.
      Hergenhan. University of Queensland Press, St Lucia,
      1972.

      Contains extensive bibliographical and textual notes,
      textual variants, and evidence for attributions;
      select bibliography.

163   SIMMONS, SAMUEL ROWE. <u>Marcus Clarke : An Annotated</u>
      <u>Checklist 1863-1972</u>. Ed. with additions L.T.
      Hergenhan. Studies in Australian Bibliography.
      Wentworth Press, Sydney, 1975.

      Detailed annotated checklists of Clarke's books and
      periodical contributions; chronological checklist
      of secondary material; short-title list of Clarke's
      books. For a selective checklist see AWW by Michael
      Wilding (forthcoming 1976).

164   ELLIOTT, BRIAN. <u>Marcus Clarke</u>. Clarendon Press,
      Oxford, 1958.

      Standard biography, although the account of Clarke's
      historical research has since been modified. Has
      useful description of manuscript holdings.

Eleanor Dark, 1901-

165   ANDERSON, HUGH. 'Eleanor Dark : A Handlist of Her
      Books and Critical References'. <u>Biblionews</u>, 1st
      series, vol. 7, no. 9, August 1954, pp. 30-33.

      Bibliographical descriptions of books; chronolog-
      ical checklist of critical references.

166   ANDERSON, HUGH. 'Eleanor Dark : A <u>Bulletin</u> Check-
      list'. <u>Biblionews and Australian Notes & Queries</u>,
      2nd series, vol. 3, no. 2, 1969, p. 20.

      A checklist of fourteen stories and nineteen poems,
      1921-46 (mostly as 'Patricia O'Rane'). Not
      restricted to <u>Bulletin</u> contributions: nine of the
      items listed were published elsewhere.

'M. Barnard Eldershaw'
(Marjorie Barnard, 1897-   and Flora Eldershaw, 1897-1956)

167   BROWN, LYN. 'Marjorie Barnard : A Checklist 1920-
      1969'. <u>Biblionews and Australian Notes & Queries</u>,
      2nd series, vol. 4, nos 3 & 4, 1970, pp. 5-9.

Eighty-five items; lists of works by Marjorie
Barnard and by 'M. Barnard Eldershaw'. Includes
stories, articles, and reviews; collaborative work
is treated in less detail. Some annotations.

168   RORABACHER, LOUISE E. Marjorie Barnard and M.
Barnard Eldershaw. TWAS. Twayne, New York, 1973.

Standard Twayne format; for a fuller and more
detailed listing of primary works, particularly
those in periodicals, see Brown (167).

R.D. FitzGerald, 1902-

169   VAN WAGENINGEN, JENNIFER & O'BRIEN, PATRICIA. R.D.
FitzGerald : A Bibliography. Bibliographies of
Australian Writers. Libraries Board of South Aust-
ralia, Adelaide, 1970.

Lists 453 items, 1920-69; indexed. Less comprehensive for poems than Anderson (170), but records
some additional details; supplemented annually in
(7), but the supplements do not incorporate the
additional poems listed by Anderson.

170   ANDERSON, HUGH. 'A Checklist of the Poems of Robert
D. FitzGerald, 1917-1965'. ALS, vol. 4, no. 3, May
1970, pp. 280-86.

Lists eighty-one poems including many published
pseudonymously; republication in FitzGerald's
books is noted and new titles recorded. Fuller
listing than (169), especially for early poems.

171   DAY, A. GROVE. Robert D. FitzGerald. TWAS. Twayne,
New York, 1974.

Standard Twayne format; uses unpublished letters.

Miles Franklin, 1879-1954

172   STONE, WALTER. 'Miles Franklin : Biography and
Bibliography'. Miles Franklin's Manuscripts and
Typescripts. Catalogue no. 47, Berkelouw, Sydney,
1962.

Includes a biography, descriptions of the books and
manuscripts in her possession at the time of her
death, and an annotated checklist of her work.

173   BARNARD, MARJORIE. Miles Franklin. Rev. and enlarged
edn. Hill of Content, Melbourne, 1967. 1st edn 1967
in TWAS.

Standard Twayne format; good biography. For a more
selective checklist see AWW by Ray Mathew (1963).

Joseph Furphy, 1843-1912

('Tom Collins')

174   STONE, WALTER W. Joseph Furphy : An Annotated
       Bibliography. Studies in Australian Bibliography.
       Stone, Cremorne, 1955.

       Bibliography of books; checklists of periodical
       publications; chronological checklist of secondary
       references.

175   LEBEDEWA, NINA. 'Furphy Criticism since 1955 : A
       Checklist'. ALS, vol. 3, no. 2, October 1967,
       pp. 149-50.

       Supplements Stone (174).

176   Kate Baker : A Guide to Her Collection in the
       National Library of Australia. Manuscript Section,
       NLA, Canberra, 1972.

       The important Furphy collection is separated from
       the material relating to Baker; the Guide includes
       an index of correspondents.

177   BARNES, JOHN. Joseph Furphy. AWW. Lansdowne,
       Melbourne, 1963.

       Useful review of biographical studies. For a more
       comprehensive Furphy bibliography see Stone (174)
       and Lebedewa (175). New edition forthcoming, 1976.

Dame Mary Gilmore, 1865-1962

178   CUSACK, DYMPHNA, MOORE, T. INGLIS & OVENDEN, BARRIE.
       Mary Gilmore : A Tribute. Australasian Book
       Society, Sydney, 1965.

       An illustrated commemorative volume; contains
       selected verse and prose, biographical material,
       and an annotated descriptive bibliography of her
       books by Walter Stone. For some periodical con-
       tributions and secondary material, see (179).

179   Dame Mary Jean Gilmore : A Bibliography. Fryer
       Library, University of Queensland, St Lucia, 1961.

       Ninety-five items; checklists of her books (1910-
       55), poems in periodicals (1940-60), stories,
       articles and reviews (1933-59) and secondary
       material (1930-60). Less comprehensive than other
       Fryer checklists.

180   A Guide to the Papers of Dame Mary Gilmore D.B.E. in
       the National Library of Australia. NLA, Canberra,
       1962.

Brief descriptions of collections of manuscript
and typescript poems, notebooks, diaries, and
correspondence.

Adam Lindsay Gordon, 1833-70

181   EHRHARDT, MARIANNE. Adam Lindsay Gordon, 1833-70 :
Bibliography. Fryer Library, University of Queensland, St Lucia, 1970.

Lists about 750 items; bibliography of books;
checklists of poems (including some published
anonymously and pseudonymously) in periodicals, and
secondary works (including many early reviews);
brief listing of manuscripts located in Brisbane.
Some annotations; index. An enlarged edition is
in preparation.

182   A Bibliography of Adam Lindsay Gordon. Commonwealth
National Library, Canberra, 1953 .

Lists 134 items, including manuscripts and papers as
well as books and secondary material. Gives a location (usually Mitchell Library) for items not in
NLA.

183   MACRAE, C.F. Adam Lindsay Gordon. TWAS. Twayne,
New York, 1968.

Standard Twayne format; uncritical biography; good
bibliography, including manuscript sources.

184   WILDE, W.H. Adam Lindsay Gordon. AWW. OUP,
Melbourne, 1972.

Bibliography usefully supplements MacRae (183) for
secondary sources, including some older items.
Both depend largely for their biographical information on Edith Humphris, The Life of Adam Lindsay
Gordon (London, 1935).

Charles Harpur, 1813-68

185   RAWLING, J. NORMINGTON. Charles Harpur, An Australian.
A & R, Sydney, 1962.

The best biography but sometimes unreliable. The
notes and bibliography are helpful but inadequate;
the bibliography does not list Harpur's periodical
contributions.

186   WRIGHT, JUDITH. <u>Charles Harpur</u>. AWW. Lansdowne,
Melbourne, 1963.

Bibliography mainly useful for secondary material;
new edition forthcoming 1976.

Xavier Herbert, 1901-

187   <u>Xavier Herbert (1901-) : Draft Bibliography, 1972,</u>
<u>with Additions to 1974</u>. Fryer Library, University
of Queensland, St Lucia, 1974.

More than 300 items; checklists of Herbert's works
(including translations), and secondary material.
For a more selective checklist see AWW by H.P.
Heseltine (1973).

A.D. Hope, 1907-

188   O'BRIEN, PATRICIA. <u>A.D. Hope : A Bibliography</u>.
Bibliographies of Australian Writers. Libraries
Board of South Australia, Adelaide, 1968.

Checklist of primary and secondary material (339
items). Hope's articles, reviews, poems are listed
in a single sequence; indexed. Supplemented
annually in (7). Unreliable; many of the important
errors and omissions were noted by Leon Cantrell,
<u>ALS</u>, vol. 5, no. 1, May 1971, pp. 87-91. Will be
superseded by Joy Hooton's <u>A.D. Hope</u> (Australian
Bibliographies; OUP, Melbourne, forthcoming 1976).

Henry Kendall, 1839-82

189   KENDALL, HENRY. <u>The Poetical Works</u>. Ed. T.T. Reed.
Libraries Board of South Australia, Adelaide, 1966.

A scholarly edition, but omitting 'ephemeral contributions, made under various pseudonyms'.
Records textual variants and gives manuscript and
printed sources.

190   <u>Henry Kendall : A Guide to his Manuscripts in the</u>
<u>National Library of Australia</u>. Manuscript Branch,
NLA, Canberra, 1965.

A descriptive list of notebooks of poems.

191   REED, T. THORNTON. <u>Henry Kendall</u>. Rigby, Adelaide,
      1960.

      Useful biographical outline; detailed bibliography
      of Kendall's books. For secondary material see
      Moore (192).

192   MOORE, T. INGLIS. 'Henry Kendall : A Bibliography'.
      <u>Biblionews</u>, 1st series, vol. 10, no. 2, February
      1957, pp. 6-9.

      An annotated list of Kendall's books, less detailed
      than Reed (191); more useful for its checklist of
      critical references.

                    Thomas Keneally, 1935-

193   <u>Thomas Michael Keneally : A Preliminary Bibliography</u>.
      Fryer Library, University of Queensland, St Lucia,
      1975.

      About 350 items; comprehensive chronological check-
      lists of primary and secondary works; index.

                    Henry Kingsley, 1830-76

194   SCHEUERLE, WILLIAM H. <u>The Neglected Brother : A
      Study of Henry Kingsley</u>. Florida State University
      Press, Tallahassee, 1971.

      The most substantial biographical study; also
      contains the best bibliography of Kingsley, good
      for early reviews but weak on recent Australian
      articles.

195   BARNES, JOHN. <u>Henry Kingsley and Colonial Fiction</u>.
      AWW. OUP, Melbourne, 1971.

      Bibliography supplements Scheuerle (194), especially
      for recent Australian criticism.

                    Henry Lawson, 1867-1922

196   LAWSON, HENRY. <u>Collected Prose</u>. Ed. Colin Roderick.
      2 vols. A & R, Sydney, 1972. Vol. 1, Short Stories
      and Sketches 1888-1922; Vol. 2, Autobiographical
      and Other Writings 1887-1922,

      Edited texts, including previously uncollected
      material, but without textual notes. A third volume
      of <u>Commentary</u>, containing the textual notes, has
      been promised.

197   LAWSON, HENRY. Collected Verse. Ed. Colin Roderick.
       3 vols. A & R, Sydney, 1967-69. Vol. 1, 1885-1900;
       Vol. 2, 1901-09; Vol. 3, 1910-22.

       A variorum edition; each volume contains a biblio-
       graphy of manuscript and printed sources.

198   LAWSON, HENRY. Letters, 1890-1922. Ed. Colin
       Roderick. A & R, Sydney, 1970.

       Includes 535 letters. Extensive notes give prove-
       nance, and background information, and often quote
       from letters to Lawson. See also (204).

199   MACKANESS, GEORGE. An Annotated Bibliography of
       Henry Lawson. A & R, Sydney, 1951.

       Detailed bibliographical descriptions of the
       editions and issues of his books, with lengthy
       annotations (sometimes anecdotal). Indexes the
       first book publication of each poem and story, and
       has a checklist of secondary material.

200   STONE, WALTER W. Henry Lawson : A Chronological
       Checklist of his Contributions to The Bulletin,
       1887-1924. Studies in Australian Bibliography.
       2nd edn. Wentworth Press, Sydney, 1964. 1st
       edn 1954.

201   NESBITT, BRUCE. 'Some Notes on Lawson's Contrib-
       utions to The Bulletin, 1887-1900'. Biblionews,
       2nd series, vol. 2, no. 1, January 1967, pp. 17-20.

       Stone lists over 400 items by Lawson and gives a
       selected list of references to him in The Bulletin.
       Nesbitt lists thirty-one items correcting and
       adding to Stone.

202   RODERICK, COLIN (ed.). Henry Lawson Criticism,
       1894-1971. A & R, Sydney, 1972.

       An anthology of selected criticism (about 115
       items) and an annotated but incomplete biblio-
       graphy. Index to both parts.

203   MATTHEWS, BRIAN. The Receding Wave : Henry
       Lawson's Prose. Melbourne University Press,
       Melbourne, 1972.

       A critical study; contains a very useful select
       bibliography which includes references to manu-
       scripts and supplements Roderick (202). For a
       much shorter checklist see AWW by Stephen Murray-
       Smith (2nd edn, 1975).

204   CHAPLIN, HARRY F. Henry Lawson : His Books, Manu-
       scripts, Autograph Letters and Association Copies,
       Together with Publications by Louisa Lawson.
       Studies in Australian Bibliography. Wentworth
       Press, Surry Hills, 1974.

The most notable items in this large collection
(229 entries) are the letters, many described for
the first time. Extensive quotations·and
annotations.

205   PROUT, DENTON. Henry Lawson : The Grey Dreamer.
       Rigby, Adelaide, 1963.

       The standard biography; thorough but unscholarly.
       For a more scholarly treatment of Lawson's life,
       see the four illustrated articles by Colin Roderick
       in the Journal of the Royal Australian Historical
       Society: vol. 45, no. 3, November 1959, pp. 105-38
       (1883-93); vol. 53, no. 2, June 1967, pp. 101-21
       (1893-96); vol. 55, no. 4, December 1969, pp.
       328-54 (1896-1900); vol. 46, no. 3, August 1960,
       pp. 123-60 (1910-18).

                    Norman Lindsay, 1879-1969

206   Norman Alfred William Lindsay : Contributions
       towards a Bibliography. Fryer Library, University
       of Queensland, St Lucia, 1963.

       About 200 items; checklist of Lindsay's books, but
       most useful for its lists of his articles and of
       secondary references.

207   CHAPLIN, HARRY F. Norman Lindsay : His Books,
       Manuscripts and Autograph Letters in the Library
       of, and Annotated by, Harry F. Chaplin. Studies
       in Australian Bibliography. Wentworth Press,
       Sydney, 1969.

       Describes 113 entries; much bibliographical
       information and extensive quotations from letters.
       Gives dates of composition deriving from Lindsay
       himself. ، The collection is now in the Fisher
       Library (294).

208   HETHERINGTON, JOHN. Norman Lindsay : The Embattled
       Olympian. OUP, Melbourne, 1973.

       The authorized biography, with a bibliography of
       Lindsay's writings and of books illustrated by
       him. The secondary material listed is mainly
       biographical. For a more selective, but sometimes
       unreliable, bibliography see AWW by Hetherington
       (3rd edn, 1969). Douglas Stewart's Norman Lindsay
       (Melbourne, 1975) contains an extensive survey of
       Lindsayana in Australian galleries and libraries.

James McAuley, 1917-

209 SMITH, VIVIAN. James McAuley. AWW. OUP, Melbourne, 1970.

Includes the best bibliography of McAuley's works and a good checklist of critical material. For more recent works and some earlier criticism see McAuley's A Map of Australian Verse : The Twentieth Century (Melbourne, 1975), pp. 217-18.

Hugh McCrae, 1876-1958

210 McCRAE, HUGH. The Letters. Selected by Robert D. FitzGerald. A & R, Sydney, 1970.

Includes 261 letters (many abridged) selected from a large correspondence. Biographical appendix and notes.

211 CHAPLIN, HARRY F. A McCrae Miscellany : Georgiana Huntly McCrae, George Gordon McCrae and Hugh Raymond McCrae; Their Books, Manuscripts, Letters and Drawings in the Library of Harry F. Chaplin. Studies in Australian Bibliography. Wentworth Press, Sydney, [1967].

Describes 153 entries. Discursive annotations, with many quotations. The collection is now in the Fisher Library (294).

Kenneth ('Seaforth') Mackenzie, 1913-55

212 MACKENZIE, KENNETH. The Poems. Eds Evan Jones & Geoffrey Little. A & R, Sydney, 1972.

A selected rather than collected edition; the textual notes are brief and usually record only previous publication. Prints 195 poems but omits many others, some of which are listed.

213 DAVIS, DIANA. 'A Checklist of Kenneth Mackenzie's Works'. ALS, vol. 4, no. 4, October 1970, pp. 398-404.

Also includes a list of critical and biographical articles and describes the most important collections of Mackenzie manuscripts. For a more selective bibliography see AWW by Evan Jones (1969).

'Furnley Maurice'

(Frank Wilmot, 1881-1942)

214   ANDERSON, HUGH & RAMSDEN, B.M. Frank Wilmot
(Furnley Maurice) : A Bibliography and a
Criticism. Melbourne University Press, Melbourne,
1955.

The bibliography contains detailed descriptions of
his books, and chronological checklists of poems,
stories, articles and reviews in periodicals, and
of biographical and critical writings about him to
1952.

John Shaw Neilson, 1872-1942

215   NEILSON, JOHN SHAW. Unpublished Poems. Ed. James
Devaney. A & R, Sydney, 1947.

Includes fifty-nine poems (since reprinted) and a
selection of fragments, rejected stanzas, and
revisions.

216   NEILSON, JOHN SHAW. Witnesses of Spring : Unpublished
Poems. Ed. Judith Wright. A & R, Sydney, 1970.

Drafts from the notebooks 'edited' into a conjectural
final form to produce a reading text. Unscholarly;
occasional annotations. For a more scholarly discussion of the problems of Neilson's text see three
articles by J.F. Burrows and others in Southerly,
vol. 32, no. 2, June 1972, pp. 118-44; vol. 33,
no. 3, September 1973, pp. 313-22; vol. 35, no. 3,
September 1975, pp. 276-93.

217   ANDERSON, HUGH. Shaw Neilson : An Annotated Bibliography and Checklist 1893-1964. Studies in Australian Bibliography. Rev. edn. Wentworth Press,
Sydney, 1964. 1st edn 1956.

Detailed descriptions of Neilson's books; checklist
of poems published in periodicals, musical settings,
manuscripts and a useful list of untraced poems;
selection of secondary material to 1962. For a more
selective checklist see AWW by H.J. Oliver (1968).

218   CHAPLIN, HARRY F. A Neilson Collection : An
Annotated Catalogue of First Editions, Inscribed
Copies, Letters, Manuscripts, and Association Items.
Studies in Australian Bibliography. Wentworth Press,
Sydney, 1964.

Contains seventy-six entries including many manuscripts and letters; extensive quotations. Now in
NLA (291).

219   ANDERSON, HUGH & BLAKE, L.J. John Shaw Neilson.
      Rigby, Adelaide, 1972.

      A detailed and illustrated biography; much new
      material on his early period. Extensive reference
      is made to manuscripts and other primary sources.
      The 'Bibliography', though actually a collection of
      notes to each chapter, is a good source for bio-
      graphical references.

220   DEVANEY, JAMES. Shaw Neilson. A & R, Sydney, 1944.

      An earlier and uncritical biography. Mainly
      valuable for two appendices which quote from
      letters, most now in the Chaplin collection (218),
      and Neilson's comments on his poems.

                  Bernard O'Dowd, 1866-1953

221   ANDERSON, HUGH. Bernard O'Dowd (1866-1953) : An
      Annotated Bibliography. Studies in Australian
      Bibliography. Wentworth Books, Sydney, 1963.

      Complete bibliography of O'Dowd's books; compre-
      hensive list of his other writings (including
      manuscripts and many pseudonymous poems); annotated
      list of articles on O'Dowd (1947-60); selected
      list of reviews.

222   ANDERSON, HUGH. The Poet Militant : Bernard O'Dowd.
      Rev. and enlarged edn. Hill of Content, Melbourne,
      1969. 1st edn 1968 in TWAS.

      Standard Twayne format though with longer biography
      than usual; most useful for O'Dowd's early life
      and work. Supplements the authorized, but undoc-
      umented, biography, Bernard O'Dowd by Victor Kennedy
      & Nettie Palmer (Melbourne, 1954). Good biblio-
      graphy, generously annotated.

                  Vance Palmer, 1885-1959 and

                  Nettie Palmer, 1885-1964

223   HOTIMSKY, C.M. & STONE, WALTER. 'A Bibliographical
      Checklist'. Meanjin, vol. 18, no. 2, July 1959,
      pp. 264-69.

      Annotated checklists of most of the Palmers' books,
      their articles in Meanjin and The Bulletin, and
      selected secondary sources. This number of Meanjin
      was a special Palmer issue.

224   Edward Vance Palmer (1885-1959) : A Bibliography.
       Fryer Library, University of Queensland, St Lucia,
       1963.

       Lists articles and reviews by Vance and secondary
       material. For a more selective checklist see AWW
       by Vivian Smith (1971).

225   SMITH, VIVIAN. 'Nettie Palmer : A Checklist of
       Literary Journalism 1918-1936'. ALS, vol. 6,
       no. 2, October 1973, pp. 190-96.

226   Nettie Palmer : A List of Articles and Book Reviews
       1930-1959. Fryer Library, University of Queensland,
       St Lucia, 1961.

       Smith lists about 280 items in chronological order,
       mainly from the Illustrated Tasmanian Mail. It is
       complemented by the Fryer checklist which separates
       articles and reviews, listing about 250 items, most
       from All About Books (1930-35).

227   Palmer Papers : A Guide to the Papers of Vance and
       Nettie Palmer Held in the National Library of
       Australia. Manuscript Section, NLA, Canberra, 1973.

       Useful guide to a very large, miscellaneous
       collection. Some parts are described in more
       detail than others; index of correspondents.

228   SMITH, VIVIAN. Vance and Nettie Palmer. TWAS.
       Twayne, New York, 1975.

       Standard Twayne format; bibliography excludes
       periodical contributions, but is the best listing
       of Nettie's books and of books for which she wrote
       introductions.

229   HESELTINE, HARRY. Vance Palmer. University of
       Queensland Press, St Lucia, 1970.

       The most substantial biography of Vance, although
       primarily a critical account of his work; select
       bibliography.

                  A.B. ('Banjo') Paterson, 1864-1941

230   OLLIF, LORNA. Andrew Barton Paterson. TWAS. Twayne,
       New York, 1971.

       Standard Twayne format; bibliography supplemented
       by Semmler (231) for manuscripts. For a more
       selective checklist see AWW by Clement Semmler (2nd
       edn, 1972).

231   SEMMLER, CLEMENT. <u>The Banjo of the Bush : The Work,</u>
      <u>Life and Times of A.B. Paterson.</u> 2nd edn.
      University of Queensland Press, St Lucia, 1974.
      1st edn 1966.

      Paterson's activities in the context of his times;
      draws on new documentary evidence and uncollected
      poems. The revised edition has some new illustrat-
      ions and a preface which draws attention to new
      biographical information and some unlisted poems.
      Except for manuscripts, Ollif (230) has a better
      bibliography.

232   STONE, WALTER W. 'Materials towards a Checklist of
      <u>Bulletin</u> Contributions by A.B. Paterson to 1902'.
      <u>Biblionews</u>, 1st series, vol. 10, no. 12, December
      1957, pp. 38-40.

      About 100 items, including a few prose pieces.

                     Hal Porter, 1911-

233   FINCH, JANETTE H. <u>Bibliography of Hal Porter.</u>
      Bibliographies of Australian Writers. Libraries
      Board of South Australia, Adelaide, 1965.

      Contains 249 items by and about Porter; indexed.
      Marred by both errors and omissions: many were
      listed in Michael Wilding's review in <u>ALS</u>, vol. 3,
      no. 2, October 1967, pp. 142-48. Supplemented
      annually in (7) but more effectively by Mary Lord,
      'A Contribution to the Bibliography of Hal Porter',
      <u>ALS</u>, vol. 4, no. 4, October 1970, pp. 405-09, which
      lists some important omissions and comprehensively
      extends the bibliography to 1968. For a more
      selective checklist see AWW by Lord (1974).

             Katharine Susannah Prichard, 1883-1969

234   THROSSELL, RIC. <u>Wild Weeds and Wind Flowers.</u> A & R,
      Sydney, 1975.

      Biography of Prichard by her son, with a checklist
      of her books (including translations) and selected
      criticism; index. For her periodical publications
      see the checklist in Jack Beasley, <u>The Rage for Life</u>
      (Sydney, 1964).

235   <u>Katharine Susannah Prichard : A Contribution Towards</u>
       <u>a Bibliography</u>. Fryer Library, University of
       Queensland, St Lucia, 1964.

       The best bibliography of Prichard, especially for
       periodical contributions and secondary material.
       For a more selective checklist see AWW by Henrietta
       Drake-Brockman (1967).

                    'Henry Handel Richardson'
               (Ethel Florence Lindesay Robertson,
                          1870-1946)

236   HOWELLS, GAY. <u>Henry Handel Richardson, 1870-1946 :</u>
       <u>A Bibliography to Honour the Centenary of Her Birth</u>.
       NLA, Canberra, 1970.

       A reliable list of all Richardson's works (including
       translations), biographical and critical work about
       her, and descriptions of principal manuscript
       holdings. For a more selective checklist see AWW
       by Vincent Buckley (2nd edn, 1970).

237   <u>Henry Handel Richardson : A Guide to Her Papers in</u>
       <u>the National Library of Australia</u>. Manuscript
       Section, NLA, Canberra, 1975.

       Brief descriptive notes with an index of corres-
       pondents.

238   GREEN, DOROTHY. <u>Ulysses Bound : Henry Handel</u>
       <u>Richardson and Her Fiction</u>. Australian National
       University Press, Canberra, 1973.

       A critical study; but with an important appendix
       discussing some personal papers recently released.
       (Further important biographical material in the
       Mitchell Library will not be available for study
       until 1996.)   There is a short biography in
       William D. Elliott, <u>Henry Handel Richardson</u> (TWAS;
       New York, 1975).

                    Kenneth Slessor, 1901-71

239   <u>Kenneth Slessor : A Bibliography</u>. Fryer Library,
       University of Queensland, St Lucia, 1975.

       Much more comprehensive than Jaffa (240), especially
       for reviews and criticism of particular poems. No
       poems later than 1967.

240   JAFFA, HERBERT C. <u>Kenneth Slessor</u>. TWAS. Twayne,
       New York, 1971.

       Standard Twayne format; thin on biography. Good
       bibliography but omitting periodical publication of
       poems. For a fuller bibliography see (239) and for
       a more selective one see AWW by Graham Burns (1975).

241   <u>Kenneth Slessor : A Guide to His Papers in the
       National Library of Australia</u>. Manuscript Section,
       NLA, Canberra, 1976.

       Summary guide to a large collection; index of
       correspondents.

Christina Stead, 1902-

242   <u>Christina Stead : A Preliminary Bibliography</u>. Fryer
       Library, University of Queensland, St Lucia, 1971.

       A checklist of primary and secondary sources,
       supplemented by Beston (243) for recent work and
       some juvenilia. For selective checklists see R.G.
       Geering's two volumes, in AWW (1969) and in TWAS
       (1969).

243   BESTON, ROSE MARIE. 'A Christina Stead Biblio-
       graphy'. <u>World Literature Written in English</u>, vol.
       15, no. 1, April 1976, pp. 96-103.

       Checklists of first English and American editions
       of her books, other writings (in classified lists),
       and secondary material.

A.G. Stephens, 1865-1933

244   No reliable bibliography; but a forthcoming
       selection of Stephens' work, edited by Leon
       Cantrell, will contain an extensive checklist
       of Stephens' writings (A & R, Sydney, 1976).

Douglas Stewart, 1913-

245   SEMMLER, CLEMENT. <u>Douglas Stewart</u>. TWAS. Twayne,
       New York, 1974.

       Standard Twayne format; the bibliography is most
       useful for recent secondary material. For an
       earlier, but fuller, bibliography see (246); for
       a more selective list see AWW by Keesing (1965).

246   <u>Douglas Alexander Stewart : A Bibliography</u>. Fryer
        Library, University of Queensland, St Lucia, 1961.

        The most comprehensive bibliography, supplemented
        by Semmler (245) for more recent work. Particularly
        useful for listings of poems, articles, reviews and
        short stories in periodicals, and reviews of
        Stewart's books.

                        Randolph Stow, 1935-

247   O'BRIEN, PATRICIA. <u>Randolph Stow : A Bibliography</u>.
        Bibliographies of Australian Writers. Libraries
        Board of South Australia, Adelaide, 1968.

        Contains 281 items; indexed; more accurate than
        others in this series but still far from compre-
        hensive. Supplemented annually in (7), by Beston
        (248), and by the Fryer list (249).

248   BESTON, ROSE MARIE. 'A Bibliography of Randolph
        Stow'. <u>Literary Half Yearly</u>, vol. 16, no. 2,
        July 1975, pp. 137-44.

        Lists only English-language hard-cover editions of
        Stow's works; excludes reviews and poems published
        in anthologies, but records periodical publication
        of uncollected poems.

249   <u>Randolph Stow (1935-)</u>. Fryer Library, University
        of Queensland, St Lucia, 1972.

        Supplements O'Brien (247) and Beston (248); lists
        all editions of Stow's books; good for poems in
        anthologies; less comprehensive than Beston for
        poems in periodicals.

                        Kylie Tennant, 1912-

250   DICK, MARGARET. <u>The Novels of Kylie Tennant</u>. Rigby,
        Adelaide, 1966.

        Critical introduction; biographical note; useful
        bibliography of her work (including reprints and
        translations) and secondary material. For a more
        complete list of Tennant's articles see (251).

251   <u>Kylie Tennant : Contributions towards a Bibliography</u>.
Fryer Library, University of Queensland, St Lucia,
1964.

Supplements Dick (250) especially for Tennant's
literary journalism.

'Price Warung'

(William Astley, 1855-1911)

252   WARUNG, PRICE. <u>Tales of the Convict System</u> :
<u>Selected Stories</u>. Ed. B.G. Andrews. University
of Queensland Press, St Lucia, 1975.

Includes textual and explanatory notes.

253   ANDREWS, BARRY. 'Price Warung : Some Bibliographical
Details'. <u>ALS</u>, vol. 3, no. 1, October 1968, pp.
290-304.

An account of the composition and publication of
Warung's stories, with a checklist of 111 stories.
For additions and corrections see Andrews' later
list (which also includes contemporary reviews and
Warung's own reviews and literary journalism), <u>ALS</u>,
vol. 7, no. 1, May 1975, pp. 95-98.

Francis Webb, 1925-73

254   <u>Francis Webb (1925-1973) Commemorative Issue</u>.
<u>Poetry Australia</u>, no. 56, September 1975.

Contains a comprehensive bibliography (compiled in
the Fryer Library) of work by and about Webb;
twelve uncollected poems (1941-73); a holograph
facsimile; memoirs and critical articles.

Patrick White, 1912-

255   LAWSON, ALAN. <u>Patrick White</u>. Australian Bibliographies. OUP, Melbourne, 1974.

A comprehensive checklist, lightly annotated, of
White's published writings and of biographical and
critical material (including incidental references).
Includes theses and some manuscripts, but not
<u>Thirteen Poems</u> [1929] which has since come to light.
Indexes to authors and to periodicals. For a more
selective checklist see AWW by Geoffrey Dutton (4th
edn, 1971).

Judith Wright, 1915-

256   O'BRIEN, PATRICIA & ROBINSON, ELIZABETH. <u>Judith Wright : A Bibliography</u>. Bibliographies of Australian Writers. Libraries Board of South Australia, Adelaide, 1968.

Lists 602 items; indexed; for many omissions see Hugh Anderson, <u>ALS</u>, vol. 3, no. 4, October 1968, pp. 312-13. Supplemented annually in (7), and in (257).

257   HOPE, A.D. <u>Judith Wright</u>. AWW. OUP, Melbourne, 1975.

Contains a particularly good bibliography.

IV   PERIODICALS

Journals have always played a particularly important role in Australian literature and literary studies. An acquaintance with the general characteristics and contents of the most important titles is therefore a necessary part of the study of Australian literature. As well as scanning the latest issues as they appear, which is always advisable, it is worth examining back runs of selected titles such as Australian Literary Studies (269), Meanjin (280), Overland (282), Quadrant (284), and Southerly (286). Among the many advantages to be gained are a better understanding of social and literary contexts, and a fuller awareness of the historical evolution of literary interests and standards. Such searches are often rewarded more tangibly by the discovery of unexpected items of intrinsic value or ephemeral interest.

The first part of this chapter describes the most useful guides to Australian periodicals of literary interest. Tregenza (261) supplements our listing for an earlier period; Green's History of Australian Literature (117) discusses newspapers and periodicals and is supplemented by the list of articles about literary magazines in Mayer (260). For 'little magazines' see Duwell (262), Australasian Small Press Review (263), and Shapcott (264).

The second part of this chapter lists the current serials (including a few which have ceased publication only recently) most likely to contain important material on Australian literature; some also contain new creative writing. Location aids for particular articles and reviews are described above (66-84).

A   Guides

258   Current Australian Serials. 9th edn. NLA, Canberra, 1975. 1st edn 1963.

Classified subject-list with details of scope, editor, address, and level of content. Indexes titles, recent former titles, and sponsoring organizations.

259   Press, Radio, and T.V. Guide : Australia, New
       Zealand, and the Pacific Islands. Country Press,
       Sydney, 1974. 1st edn 1914. Title has varied.

       Geographical arrangement for newspapers; classif-
       ied list of periodicals, less detailed than Current
       Australian Serials (258).

260   MAYER, HENRY. Bibliographical Notes on the Press in
       Australia and Related Subjects. Department of
       Government and Public Administration, University of
       Sydney, Sydney, 1963.

       A working guide rather than a bibliography, but
       contains much very useful information about news-
       papers and periodicals. Lists bibliographies,
       indexes (some in newspaper offices), directories,
       theses, and articles. There is also an incomplete
       but valuable listing of 'little' and literary
       magazines, 1857-1963.

261   TREGENZA, JOHN. Australian Little Magazines, 1923-
       1954 : Their Role in Forming and Reflecting Literary
       Trends. Libraries Board of South Australia,
       Adelaide, 1964.

       Brief history of literary magazines (not always
       'little') in the period; chronological bibliography
       of Australian 'little' magazines 1923-54, with
       details of frequency, editors, characteristic
       content, important contributors. Lists forty-nine
       periodicals: there were many others. Not always
       reliable in detail but a useful source.

262   DUWELL, MARTIN. 'A Guide to Australian Literary
       Magazines.' SPAN, no. 2, April 1976, pp. 40-48.

       Critical survey, with emphasis on magazines
       publishing creative writing. Lists editorial
       addresses of the twenty-six magazines discussed.

263   Australasian Small Press Review. Manly, N.S.W.,
       1975- . Three times yearly.

       Includes 'Small Press Record', a useful guide to
       Australian 'little magazines' with addresses and
       interests of current titles. A fuller, but un-
       annotated, list of serials publishing poetry
       appeared in No. 2, 1975. Although 'Small Press
       Record' is incomplete, it is the most useful guide
       to a difficult field: 'little magazines' are
       often irregular and poorly distributed.

264   SHAPCOTT, TOM.   'Australian Literary Magazines'.
       Makar, vol. 7, no. 3, November 1971, pp. 34-36.

       An earlier compilation valuable for its descriptions
       of some magazines no longer current. The annotat-
       ions comment on the kind and quality of poetry
       usually published.

B   Individual titles

265   AUMLA. Australasian Universities Language and
       Literature Association (AULLA), Townsville,
       1953- . Twice yearly. Place of publication
       varies.

       Some critical and scholarly articles, many reviews.
       Not confined to English studies: a few articles on
       Australian topics. Annual index. AULLA also
       publishes a twice-yearly Newsletter (1962-).
       This contains notes and news that are often of
       interest.

266   The Australian Author. Australian Society of Authors
       (ASA), Sydney, 1969- . Quarterly.

       Articles of interest to authors on books and
       writing; lists new books by members; annual list
       of members (currently over 1,200). The Society is
       a professional association working in the interests
       of authors. It has published A Guide to Book
       Contracts (Rev. edn, Sydney, 1973) and The Austral-
       ian and New Zealand Writers Handbook (Sydney, 1975).

267   Australian Book Review. Adelaide, 1961-74. Monthly
       to 1971, then quarterly. 'ABR'.

       Reviewed a wide range of books of Australian interest;
       scale of treatment varied from brief notices to
       review-articles. Other valuable features included
       regular articles on the book trade and a lively forum
       for correspondents. Also published an annual
       Children's Book and Educational Supplement (1961-70).

268   Australian Letters. Adelaide, 1957-68. Quarterly.

       A good journal of creative and critical writing;
       also paid attention to the other arts. Perhaps most
       notable for its author-artist collaborations, 1960-
       68. Some of the best contributions were collected
       by two of the editors, Max Harris and Geoffrey
       Dutton, in The Vital Decade (Melbourne, 1968).

269   Australian Literary Studies. St Lucia, 1963-
      Twice yearly. 'ALS'.

      The most important periodical in the field.
      Articles of criticism, scholarship, and literary
      history; notes and documents; 'Annual Biblio-
      graphy' (5); extensive (but not exhaustive) two-
      yearly listing of 'Research in Progress'; reviews
      scholarly and critical books but not creative
      writing. In ALS the emphasis is on scholarship and
      literary history. This emphasis is complemented by
      Southerly's (286) concentration on articles of
      literary criticism and Meanjin's (280) special
      interest in general cultural issues. These emphases
      are not, of course, exclusive.

270   Australian Studies Booklist. Sydney, 1974- .
      Irregular. 'ASB'.

      Concerned with Australian Studies, especially
      interdisciplinary topics; articles also on
      reference sources. Lists books for sale in
      Australian studies.

271   Biblionews and Australian Notes & Queries. Book
      Collectors Society of Australia, Cremorne, 1947-
      Quarterly. 1st Series 1947-64; 2nd Series 1966-
      Now irregular.

      Articles on Australiana, book-collecting, biblio-
      graphy; reviews; notes and queries; quarterly
      list of important Mitchell Library accessions;
      bibliographies and checklists. Much miscellaneous
      information; no index.

272   Bookmark. Australian Libraries Promotion Council,
      Melbourne, 1973- . Annual.

      Directory and diary containing much miscellaneous
      information of interest; lists associations,
      literary awards, useful addresses, Nobel Prize
      winners for literature, printing measures,
      publishers; notes on copyright.

273   The Bulletin. Australian Consolidated Press, Sydney,
      1880- .

      Long regarded as the most influential Australian
      magazine, especially through its 'Red Page'.
      Noted for its promotion of the 'nationalist' school
      of Australian writers. Had declined as a magazine
      of literary interest by about 1961 (the end of
      Douglas Stewart's period as literary editor); now
      a very different magazine. Microfilms of an index
      compiled in The Bulletin office (1880-1962, with
      some gaps) are held in some libraries. An annual
      index was published, 1963-65). For books published
      by The Bulletin (including anthologies selected
      from it) see George Mackaness & Walter W. Stone,

The Books of 'The Bulletin' 1880-1952 : An Annotated
Bibliography (Sydney, 1955). There are checklists
of the Bulletin contributions of Dark (166), Lawson
(200-01), and Paterson (232). See also A.G.
Stephens (244).

274 Elizabethan Theatre Trust News. Sydney, 1971-
Quarterly.

Articles, notes, and reviews on the theatre in
Australia. Some book reviews. A change of title
to Theatrescope has been announced for June 1976.

275 Journal of Commonwealth Literature. London, 1965-
Three times yearly; frequency has varied. 'JCL'.

Critical articles and reviews on Commonwealth
literature in English. Publishes 'Annual Bibliography' in geographical divisions, see also (6).

276 Komos. Clayton, 1967-73. Quarterly.

Articles and reviews on drama and theatre; Australian subjects are well-represented. Several playscripts were issued as supplements. A separate
Index was published (1973).

277 LiNQ. Townsville, 1971- . Quarterly.

Creative writing, and critical articles on contemporary literature; good coverage of Australian
subjects.

278 Makar. St Lucia, 1962- . Three times yearly.

Mainly poetry; some short stories and articles.
Particularly useful for its reviews of recent books
of poetry, and interviews (1973-) with poets.

279 Masque. Sydney, 1967-71. Six times yearly.

Articles and reviews on the performing arts (mainly
in Australia); illustrated. The gap left by
Masque may be partially filled by a new monthly
journal, Theatre Australia, which has been announced
for August 1976.

280 Meanjin Quarterly. Melbourne, 1940- . Quarterly.
Title has varied: Meanjin Papers (1940-46);
Meanjin (1947-60); Meanjin Quarterly (1961-).

Meanjin and Southerly (286) have been the two most
important journals to chart and influence the
emergence and development of modern Australian
literature and literary studies, both publishing
creative and critical writing of a high standard.
Meanjin is most notable for its continuing concern
with general and literary problems in Australia
and for articles on literature, the arts, history,

and current affairs. Indexed annually. Meanjin
Quarterly Index (1940-1965) by Marjorie Tipping
(Melbourne, 1969) is unreliable and inconveniently
classified. Several articles on Meanjin have
appeared in its pages, some by C.B. Christesen
(editor, 1940-74). See also A.M. Gibbs, Journal of
Commonwealth Literature, vol. 1 , no. 4, December
1967, pp. 130-38. Christesen also edited On Native
Grounds (Sydney, 1968), an anthology from Meanjin.

281   New Poetry. Poetry Society of Australia, Sydney,
       1954- . Six times yearly. Formerly Prism (1954-
       60) and Poetry Magazine (1961-71).

       Mainly poetry with some short critical articles and
       reviews. Less conservative than Poetry Australia
       (283), though many poets publish in both. 'Notes
       and Comments' gives brief attention to new public-
       ations and events in modern poetry (mainly Austral-
       ian).

282   Overland. Melbourne, 1954- . Quarterly.

       Creative writing, literary criticism, reviews, and
       articles on general culture and current affairs.
       Had a reputation for being leftist but was never
       exclusively so, though it has paid more attention
       to social-realist writers than other major journals.
       Its editor, Stephen Murray-Smith, compiled an
       anthology, An Overland Muster (Brisbane, 1965).

283   Poetry Australia. Sydney, 1964- . Quarterly.

       Mainly poetry; some articles and reviews. Not
       exclusively concerned with Australian poetry.
       Annual index.

284   Quadrant. Australian Association for Cultural
       Freedom, Sydney, 1956- . Formerly quarterly; monthly
       since June 1975.

       Creative writing; criticism and reviews, some of
       literary interest, others on the arts or (increas-
       ingly) current affairs. Tends to be conservative.

285   Realist. National Council of Realist Writers'
       Groups, Sydney, 1958-70. Quarterly. Formerly
       Realist Writer (1958-64).

       Mainly creative writing; articles and reviews on
       Australian literature. Often polemical, topical,
       or para-political.

286   Southerly. Sydney Branch of the English Association,
       Sydney, 1939- . Quarterly.

       Critical and creative writing; notes and news;
       reviews of creative writing and critical books;
       'Australian Writers in Profile' (1968-), a series
       of interviews and personal statements. For an
       assessment see S.E. Lee, Southerly, vol. 34, no. 2,
       1974, pp. 112-41.

287 <u>Southern Review</u>. Adelaide, 1963- . Three times
yearly.

Articles and reviews on literature in English
(including Australian); poems and short fiction.
Not to be confused with the American <u>Southern Review</u>.

288 <u>SPAN</u>. South Pacific Association for Commonwealth
Literature and Language Studies (SPACLALS), St
Lucia, 1975- . Twice yearly.

Concerned with Commonwealth literature, including
Australian. Notes on publications, conferences,
work in progress, grants, courses, research resources
and other news. Reviews books not widely noticed;
surveys of library holdings in the field.

289 <u>Westerly</u>. Perth, 1956- . Quarterly.

Creative writing and reviews; critical articles on
Australian literature, cultural matters, and current
affairs.

290 <u>World Literature Written in English</u>. Modern Language
Association of America, Group 12, Arlington, Texas,
1966- . Twice yearly. Formerly <u>Conference on
British Commonwealth Literature Newsletter</u> ('<u>CBCL</u>');
1962-66. '<u>WLWE</u>'.

Mainly notes and news; reviews and commentaries;
some critical articles and interviews.

All Australian state and university libraries have
sizeable collections of Australian literature, although
some are naturally much larger than others. The purpose
of this chapter is not to describe or compare such general
collections but to draw attention to notable strengths,
especially in unique materials such as manuscripts, archives
and formed collections. Only material of Australian
literary interest is included here.

This chapter has been compiled largely from information
supplied by librarians in response to a circular letter sent
in December 1975. A library listed here as having a strength
in a particular author, will usually possess manuscripts and
correspondence as well as first and early editions. A large
number of collections in university and other libraries
have been briefly described in the Guide to Collections of
Manuscripts Relating to Australia (59). For Australian
literary manuscripts located in British repositories see
(60).

Professional librarians can be of great assistance in
study and research. The Australian Library Journal (1951-
monthly except January; fortnightly from June 1976)
published by the Library Association of Australia and
addressed primarily to librarians, is sometimes of interest
to researchers, notably for its reviews of reference books.
More technical and specialized, but still of occasional
interest, are two journals published by sections of the
Library Association of Australia : Archives and Manuscripts
(1956-) and Australian Academic and Research Libraries
(1970-), both quarterly.

291   National Library of Australia, Canberra.

Since 1911 the Library has been entitled to a copy
of every Australian publication; this deposit
collection has been augmented by the acquisition of
the libraries of E.A. Petherick, Sir John Ferguson,
Vance and Nettie Palmer, Frank Dalby Davison,
Lloyd Ross and others. The Library has a good
collection of Australian literary manuscripts.
There are descriptive guides to the collections
of the Poetry Society of Australia; Kate Baker
(176), notable for its Furphy material; Mary
Gilmore (180); Henry Kendall (190); Vance and
Nettie Palmer (227); Henry Handel Richardson (237);
and Kenneth Slessor (241). There are also less
detailed notes available on material relating to
Barcroft Boake, C.J. Dennis, George Essex Evans,
Miles Franklin, Xavier Herbert, Hugh McCrae,

Kenneth Mackenzie, Shaw Neilson, and Bernard O'Dowd.
The manuscript collection also includes the records
of the Australian Society of Authors and the papers
of Louis Becke, Rolf Boldrewood, Christopher
Brennan, David Campbell, Gavin Casey, Nancy Cato,
Frank Clune, Dymphna Cusack, Frank Dalby Davison,
Frank Hardy, Gwen Harwood, Alan Marshall, John
Morrison, Sir Walter Murdoch, Katharine Susannah
Prichard, Roland Robinson, Steele Rudd, Tom
Shapcott, James Brunton Stephens, Douglas Stewart,
Dal Stivens, Randolph Stow, Ethel Turner, Chris
Wallace-Crabbe, and Judah Waten. An Acquisitions
Newsletter (1970- ; 5 or 6 times yearly) lists
important accessions of manuscripts and rare books.
C.A. Burmester's Guide to the Collections (Vol. 1,
Canberra, 1974) lists about 400 of the Library's
more important strengths in both book and non-book
material in many fields. Its usefulness is impaired
by an inadequate index.

292   Australian National University Library, Canberra.

Has a collection of the manuscripts and correspondence of A.D. Hope including copies or drafts
of published and unpublished works by Hope and
other authors (including Christopher Brennan,
Vincent Buckley, David Campbell, James McAuley, and
Harold Stewart). The Library also has some correspondence of Flexmore Hudson.

293   Mitchell Library, State Library of New South Wales,
Sydney.

Has the world's largest collection of Australian
literature. Among the most important author-
collections are those of Christopher Brennan, Miles
Franklin, Joseph Furphy, Mary Gilmore, Henry
Kendall, Henry Lawson, Kenneth Mackenzie, Shaw
Neilson, Henry Handel Richardson, A.G. Stephens and
P.R. Stephensen. There are less extensive collections of Rolf Boldrewood, Marcus Clarke, Charles
Harpur, Norman Lindsay, Hugh McCrae, Furnley
Maurice, Bernard O'Dowd, A.B. Paterson, Ethel
Turner, and Price Warung. Another important
resource is the collection of the correspondence
and manuscripts of the publishers Angus & Robertson.
There is a Catalogue of Manuscripts of Australasia
and the Pacific (2 vols, Sydney, 1967-69). Arranged
in two series: Series A for manuscripts catalogued
1945-63, Series B 1963-67. Inconveniently arranged
and unreliably indexed. It is not easy to assemble
all material relating to a particular author. The
entries themselves (once found) are concise but
helpful. Recent accessions are recorded in the
Report of the Council of the Library of New South
Wales. The Library's Dictionary Catalog of Printed
Books (53) is an invaluable guide.

294   Fisher Library, University of Sydney.

Strong in Australiana; special collections of
Robert Close, Frank Hardy, Henry Lawson, Norman
Lindsay, Hugh McCrae, Craig McGregor, and Dal
Stivens. There are also some unpublished plays.

295   University of New South Wales Library, Kensington.

Some correspondence and papers of Frank Clune.

296   University of New England Library, Armidale.

Most important is the Campbell Howard Collection
of unpublished Australian plays of which there is
a published catalogue (23).

297   La Trobe Library, State Library of Victoria,
Melbourne.

The Australian Manuscripts Collection has papers of
Marcus Clarke, Frank Clune, R. H. Croll, Joseph
Furphy, Rex Ingamells, Victor Kennedy, Bernard
O'Dowd, A.A. Phillips, Steele Rudd, Percival Serle,
Charles Thatcher, Henry Gyles Turner, the Australian
Literature Society (1901-52), the Australian Poetry
Lovers' Society (1934-73), and the Bread and Cheese
Club. In the J.K. Moir Collection are papers of
Miles Franklin, Mary Gilmore, Ian Mudie and Ambrose
Pratt. A Catalogue of the Manuscripts, Letters,
Documents, etc. in the Private Collection of the
State Library of Victoria (Melbourne, 1961) some-
times contains information not in the Guide to
Collections of Manuscripts Relating to Australia
(59). For recent acquisitions see the La Trobe
Library Journal (1968- ; twice yearly). The
Library also has an important collection of
historical drawings, paintings, and photographs.

298   Baillieu Library, University of Melbourne, Parkville.

Of major importance to researchers was the Library's
acquisition of the Meanjin Archive (1975). This
contains original manuscripts and corrected proofs,
correspondence with contributors, and administrative
records for the period 1940-75.

299   John Oxley Library, State Library of Queensland,
Brisbane.

Good Queensland collection; notable manuscript
holdings of Randolph Bedford and Rosa Campbell
Praed. A descriptive list of the Campbell Praed
papers is available.

300 <u>Fryer Memorial Library, University of Queensland,</u>
<u>St Lucia.</u>

A comprehensive collection of Australian literature.
The Hayes Collection is particularly notable (a
catalogue of its manuscripts is forthcoming 1976).
The Library has much of the later correspondence of
A.G. Stephens, and the papers of George Essex
Evans, Ernestine Hill and James Brunton Stephens.
There are also some papers of John Blight, Martin
Boyd and the à Beckett family, Michael Dransfield,
Mary Gilmore, Paul Grano, Rodney Hall, Gwen
Harwood, Xavier Herbert, David Rowbotham, Tom
Shapcott, and others. There is a catalogue of the
Hanger Collection of Australian playscripts (24).
The Fryer Library also maintains the index which is
the basis of the 'Annual Bibliography' published in
<u>ALS</u> (5). More comprehensive than the published
bibliography, it includes entries for individual
poems and short stories, and for many authors not
included in the 'Annual Bibliography'. The file was
begun in the 1950s; its present comprehensiveness
dates from about 1967. The entries for many authors
have been cumulated into typed lists. Some are
described in Chapter III.

301 <u>State Library of South Australia</u>, Adelaide.

Manuscripts of published works (many from Rigby
Ltd); papers of a few South Australian authors,
including Catherine Helen Spence; some interviews
and photographs of literary interest. Accessions
to the South Australian Collection are reported in
<u>South Australiana</u> (1962- ; twice yearly);
archival accessions are listed in the <u>Annual Report</u>
of the Libraries Board of South Australia. The
Library's Reference Services section operates a
bibliographical research service.

302 <u>Barr Smith Library, University of Adelaide</u>.

Small collections of the papers of Nancy Cato and
Clement Semmler.

303 <u>Flinders University of South Australia Library</u>,
<u>Bedford Park.</u>

Correspondence and papers of Rex Ingamells.

304 <u>J.S. Battye Library, State Library of Western</u>
<u>Australia</u>, Perth.

A collection of literary Western Australiana,
including manuscripts, letters, and papers. An
index of reviews of such literature is maintained.

305 <u>Murdoch University Library</u>, Murdoch, W.A.

Collections of Sir Walter Murdoch and John Boyle
O'Reilly.

VI   LITERARY STUDIES

The study of Australian literature has its own particular problems and preoccupations, but it shares its theory
and methodology with the study of other literature. Few
of the works listed in this chapter deal directly with
Australian literature, but all are relevant in a substantial
if indirect way to its study.

A   Guides to literary study and research

Practice is probably the most effective way to learn
about research, but the collective experience of the
writers of these guides is well worth taking advantage of.
To read (or at least to sample) them all is also to gain
valuable insight into the theory and practice of literary
research as seen by different minds trained in different
academic traditions: all four are distinguished scholars
in their own right.

306   THORPE, JAMES. Literary Scholarship : A Handbook
      for Advanced Students of English and American
      Literature. Houghton, Boston, 1964.

      A good introduction to serious literary study,
      addressed to English majors as well as to honours
      and postgraduate students.

307   ALTICK, RICHARD D. The Art of Literary Research.
      Norton, New York, 1963.

      More advanced than Thorpe (306): addressed
      primarily to the postgraduate student. Combines
      practical advice about research methods with
      more general reflections on the problems and
      principles of literary study. A useful section
      of 'Exercises' (pp. 221-55) is designed to give
      practice in the use of reference works. A new
      edition appeared in 1975.

308   WATSON, GEORGE. The Literary Thesis : A Guide to
      Research. Longman, London, 1970.

      By contrast with Thorpe (306) and Altick (307),
      Watson reflects British rather than American
      conditions and therefore concentrates on the thesis
      itself. Part 1 gives advice to the prospective
      postgraduate student; Part 2 reprints eight short
      pieces (not by Watson) relevant to various aspects
      of scholarly study.

309   BATESON, F.W. <u>The Scholar-Critic : An Introduction
       to Literary Research</u>. Routledge, London, 1972.

       Perhaps the most stimulating of these books; many
       lively examples of the scholar-critic's problems
       and of ways of overcoming them.

310   ALTICK, RICHARD D. <u>The Scholar Adventurers</u>.
       Macmillan, New York, 1950.

       An entertaining book about the literary researcher
       in action; lively accounts of some remarkable
       scholarly investigations (and good-luck stories)
       of the first half of this century.

B   <u>Literary criticism</u>

       There is no general agreement about what literary
criticism does, or ought to do. The works listed here
illustrate a variety of approaches to the theory and
practice of criticism.

311   WIMSATT, WILLIAM K., JR. & BROOKS, CLEANTH.
       <u>Literary Criticism : A Short History</u>. Routledge,
       London, 1957.

       A stimulating history of criticism from Aristophanes
       to Jung; it received mixed reviews. Each chapter
       is followed by a brief 'Supplement' of extracts from
       critical writings.

312   WATSON, GEORGE. <u>The Literary Critics : A Study of
       English Descriptive Criticism</u>. 2nd edn, Penguin,
       Harmondsworth, 1973. 1st edn 1962.

       A critical survey from Dryden to about 1950. More
       recent developments (in England and elsewhere) are
       discussed in Watson's <u>The Study of Literature</u> (315).

313   WELLEK, RENE & WARREN, AUSTIN. <u>Theory of Literature</u>.
       3rd edn. Harcourt, New York, 1956. 1st edn 1949.

       Should be required reading: discusses the nature
       and function of literature and literary study;
       considers various 'extrinsic' approaches to liter-
       ature; and offers a conceptual framework for the
       'intrinsic' study of literature. There is a
       comprehensive (though now rather dated) biblio-
       graphy.

314   FRYE, NORTHROP. 'Literary Criticism'. The Aims
      and Methods of Scholarship in Modern Languages
      and Literatures. Ed. James Thorpe. 2nd edn.
      Modern Language Association of America, New York,
      1970. 1st edn 1963.

      A brief (13 pp.) but satisfying essay, although
      necessarily rather abstract.

315   WATSON, GEORGE. The Study of Literature. Allen
      Lane, London, 1969.

      Watson calls the book 'a rationale of literary
      history' (p. 9). Like Wellek & Warren (313), he
      argues for an 'intrinsic' approach to literature
      that at the same time brings to bear as many
      disciplines as possible in its support.

316   KIERNAN, BRIAN. Criticism. AWW. OUP, Melbourne,
      1974.

      A critical survey of the issues implicitly or
      explicitly underlying writings about Australian
      literature by Australian critics. Has a useful
      bibliography, including a list of important
      periodicals.

C   Literary biography

      Literary biography differs in approach and emphasis
rather than in kind from political or intellectual biography: it is in biography that literary study approaches
closest to the methods and techniques of history. Much
less has been written about biography than about other
branches of literary study, perhaps because biographical
problems lend themselves less to generalization than-
critical ones. But some eminent practising biographers
have written on their art; much can also be learned from
the biographies they have written.

317   CLIFFORD, JAMES L. (ed.). Biography as an Art :
      Selected Criticism 1560-1960. OUP, London, 1962.

      A collection of essays and extracts representing
      a wide range of opinion, with a bibliography of
      twentieth-century writings on biography.

318   EDEL, LEON. Literary Biography. Hart-Davis,
      London, 1957.

      Brief discussion of the problems and methods of
      the literary biographer. Edel has written a large-
      scale life of Henry James.

319   ELLMANN, RICHARD. <u>Golden Codgers : Biographical</u>
       <u>Speculations</u>. OUP, London, 1973.

       A general essay on 'Literary Biography' followed
       by essays on individual figures (Wilde, Yeats,
       George Eliot, and others). Ellmann has written
       the standard biography of James Joyce.

D   Bibliography and textual criticism

     Bibliography is the study of books as material objects;
textual criticism is the study of the transmission of texts.
Copying and reprinting inevitably introduces errors;
textual criticism seeks to identify (and where possible to
rectify) them, usually employing bibliographical evidence in
the process. Neither study need have anything to do with
literature, although naturally it is most often literary
texts that are thought important enough to be worth investig-
ating. Three distinct kinds of activity are involved in
bibliographical and textual studies: 'enumerative' bibliography, 'analytical' bibliography, and 'critical' bibliography or textual criticism.

     Enumerative bibliography is the making of lists of
books or other bibliographical references. The making of
such lists is a basic and frequent activity in literary
research; this book is in part an enumerative bibliography.
Such compilations are properly called checklists to distinguish them from bibliographies that detail the physical make-
up of books. An enumerative bibliography or checklist will
normally give only sufficient information to enable its
contents to be unambiguously identified and located. For
modern books, author, title, and imprint are usually
sufficient. This information is conventionally presented
in a consistent form throughout a bibliography; various
styles in common use will be found in the style manuals
listed below (326-28). Some of the basic tools of
enumerative bibliography are listed in Chapter I.

     Analytical bibliography involves the close study of
the physical make-up of a book with a view to determining
its printing and publishing history. Concealed editions
are thus sometimes revealed, occasionally with unsuspected
and important changes in the text of the work.

     The textual critic uses the evidence of the analytical
bibliographer (the two may be the same person) to determine,
as far as the evidence permits, what the author wrote or
intended. The author's intentions may have been perverted
or confused through the carelessness or even the wilfulness
of printer or publisher. Sometimes the process is as
simple as restoring readings from an author's manuscript,
when the published edition has been corrupted by careless
printing or proofreading, or by the publisher's inter-
ference. Critics should exercise caution in the use of

unedited texts, especially those of earlier periods.
Small misprints can generate large blunders. Generally
speaking, when a book is reprinted without careful
editorial scrutiny, misprints will be introduced; over
several reprintings the number of such errors may become
very large.

The aim of the textual critic may be to edit a text,
or simply to examine a textual problem. In either case he
will begin with a study of the text in all its available
forms. In the course of this study, he may turn up
valuable evidence about the author's process of composition:
rough drafts or corrected proof sheets often reveal a good
deal about an author's methods and habits. Such evidence
will be of interest for its own sake in an 'author at
work' study. The textual critic who aims to produce a text
of the work under investigation may opt for one of two
basic kinds of text, 'definitive' or 'reading'. This
distinction is elaborated by Bowers (324).

320   GASKELL, PHILIP. A New Introduction to Bibliography.
       Clarendon Press, Oxford, 1972.

       An introduction to the processes of printing and
       their relevance to literary study. Gaskell
       necessarily skims over much of the ground, but his
       extensive bibliography provides a key to more
       detailed and specialized studies. Gaskell's
       predecessor, R.B. McKerrow's Introduction to Biblio-
       graphy for Literary Students (Oxford, 1927) remains
       a classic of scholarship.

321   BOWERS, FREDSON. Principles of Bibliographical
       Description. Princeton University Press, Princeton,
       1949.

       The standard work on analytical bibliography:
       how to examine and describe the physical make-up
       of a book.

322   CARTER, JOHN. ABC for Book Collectors. 5th edn.
       Hart-Davis MacGibbon, London, 1972. 1st edn 1952.
       Reprinted with corrections 1974.

       A dictionary of the technical terms most commonly
       encountered in bibliography. Although written for
       the collector, it is as useful to the student.
       Lively, witty, and trenchant, it can be read
       straight through.

323   BOWERS, FREDSON. 'Textual Criticism'. The Aims
       and Methods of Scholarship in Modern Languages
       and Literatures. Ed. James Thorpe. 2nd edn.
       Modern Language Association of America, New York,
       1970. 1st edn 1963.

       Probably the best short account of the subject,
       succinct but precise and wide-ranging.

324   BOWERS, FREDSON. 'Practical Texts and Definitive
       Editions'. In <u>Two Lectures on Editing</u> : Shakes-
       peare and Hawthorne (with Charlton Hinman). Ohio
       State University Press, Columbus, 1969.

       Distinguishes 'practical' reading texts from
       'definitive' editions. Although the examples are
       mostly drawn from Hawthorne, the argument has a
       general relevance.

325   THORPE, JAMES. <u>Principles of Textual Criticism</u>.
       Huntington Library, San Marino, 1972.

       A searching and stimulating examination of received
       opinion. Thorpe insists on textual criticism as a
       critical activity, demanding both intelligence and
       the constant exercise of aesthetic judgement.

E   Style manuals and writing aids

     In <u>The Literary Thesis</u> (308), George Watson drily
observes that in critical writing 'the reader will naturally ask whether the critic's own use of language entitles
him to be heard with respect when he speaks of the language
of others (pp. 46-47). Stylistic distinction is not easy
to acquire, but a minimum requirement in critical writing
is surely that it should avoid positive errors; that it
should be clear and unambiguous; and that references and
bibliographical information should be presented exactly and
consistently.

     Most publishers have their own 'house style' and will
copy-edit what they publish to conform to it. But many
academic journals expect authors to submit typescripts in
accordance with a specified style, and most universities
require theses to follow certain conventions of presentation. This demand is often made even of student essays.
Whatever system an author or student is required (or
decides) to use, the following works will all be found to
contain helpful advice and guidance about writing and
style. Bateson (309) and Thorpe (306) are also worth
consulting on matters of scholarly style and presentation.

326   <u>Style Manual for Authors, Editors and Printers of
       Australian Government Publications</u>. 2nd edn.
       Australian Government Publishing Service, Canberra,
       1972. 1st edn 1966.

       Actually much more than a style manual, and of
       wider usefulness than its title suggests. Con-
       tains advice on writing and editing as well as on
       presentation and preparation for printing; also
       serves as an introduction to the processes of
       printing. Its rules for bibliographical entries
       have been followed in this book. A third edition
       is in preparation.

327   <u>A Manual of Style</u>. 12th edn. University of Chicago
       Press, Chicago, 1969. 1st edn 1906.

       Based on the University of Chicago Press's own
       style, a thorough treatment of all the stages and
       problems involved in writing, printing, and revising
       books. Its recommendations are condensed for
       student use in Kate L. Turabian, <u>A Manual for</u>
       <u>Writers of Term Papers, Theses, and Dissertations</u>
       (4th edn, Chicago, 1973).

328   <u>The MLA Style Sheet</u>. 2nd edn. Modern Language
       Association of America, New York, 1970. 1st edn
       1951.

       Sets out a standard style for the documentation
       and the presentation of scholarly writing in the
       humanities. Its recommendations have been widely
       adopted by journals and academic presses in the
       United States. Much briefer than the Chicago
       <u>Manual of Style</u> (327), its primary concern is with
       the final tidying-up of scholarly manuscripts.

329   COLLINS, F. HOWARD. <u>Authors and Printers Dictionary</u>.
       11th edn, rev. Stanley Beale. OUP, London, 1973.
       1st edn 1905.

       A useful desk-compendium for settling matters of
       detail such as abbreviations, spelling, proper
       names, Latin phrases.

330   McKERROW, R.B. 'Form and Matter in the Presentation
       of Research'. <u>Review of English Studies</u>, vol. 16,
       no. 61, January 1940, pp. 116-21.

       Brief and trenchant advice on academic writing;
       McKerrow had been editor of the <u>Review of English</u>
       <u>Studies</u> since 1925 and drew on this experience for
       his discussion of the virtues and faults of
       scholarly writing. The essay has been reprinted
       in Watson's <u>The Literary Thesis</u> (308) and elsewhere.

331   GOWERS, SIR ERNEST. The <u>Complete Plain Words</u>. New
       edn, rev. Sir Bruce Fraser. Her Majesty's Stationery
       Office, London, 1973. 1st edn 1954.

       Originally written to help civil servants improve
       their official prose style; has at least as much
       to say to foggy academic writing.

332   FOWLER, H.W. <u>A Dictionary of Modern English Usage</u>.
       2nd edn, rev. Sir Ernest Gowers. Clarendon Press,
       Oxford, 1965. 1st edn 1926.

       Useful and often witty advice on points of usage
       and style; idiosyncratic and now rather conserv-
       ative in relation to current usage. Many of the
       battles Fowler was fighting have been lost; but
       the book will still resolve many problems, and is
       a delight to dip into.

333 Webster's New Dictionary of Synonyms. Merriam,
Springfield, 1968. 1st edn 1942.

Illustrates different shades of meaning and
distinguishes between words easily confused.
Many of its quotations are from literary sources.
Reflects American rather than British usage.

INDEX

References are to entries (e.g. 103) or to pages (e.g. p. 64)

Authors

Titles and Subjects